TeeJay Publishers

TJ Publishers

Advantage Business Centre

132-134 Great Ancoats Street

Manchester

M4 6DE

Tel: 0141 880 6839

Fax: 0870 124 9189

e-mail: teejaypublishers@btinternet.com

web page: www.teejaypublishers.co.uk

Printed by :-

Elanders Ltd
Merlin Way
New York Business Park
North Tyneside NE27 0QG
Registered in England number 3788582
 http://www.elanders.com/uk

Year 4 Textbook

Book 4

Produced by members of the TeeJay Writing Group

T Strang, J Geddes and J Cairns.

Front and Back Cover designed by *Fraser McKie.*
(http://www.frasermckie.com)

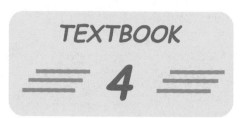

TEXTBOOK
4

National Curriculum TextBook 4

- This book covers every outcome of the **Year 4** course, as laid out in the National Curriculum England Framework Document, (September 2013).

- There are no A and B exercises. The book covers the entire **Year 4 course** without the teacher having to pick and choose which questions to leave out and which exercises are important. They all are !

- The book follows on directly from **TeeJay's Year 3 Book** and includes revision and consolidation of the work covered in the Year 3 course.

- The Year 4 Book contains a 9 page "**Chapter Zero**" which primarily revises every topic from the Year 3 course and can be used as a diagnostic tool. This could be followed by **TeeJay's** diagnostic assessments* of the work covered in our Year 3 book.

- It also contains a **Chapter 22** which revises every topic from the **Year 4** course, prior to an end of year assessment.

- Non-calculator skills are emphasised and encouraged throughout the book.

- Each chapter will have a "**Revisit - Review - Revise**" exercise as a summary.

- **Homework***, mirroring exercise by exercise, the topics in this book, is available as a photocopiable pack.

- **TeeJay's Assessment Pack*** for Year 4 work, is also available as a photocopiable pack, and can be used topic by topic or combined to form a series of Year 4 Cumulative Tests. It also contains a series of longer assessments covering the Outcomes as laid out in the **National Curriculum England framework document** (Sept 2013).

We **make** no apologies for the **multiplicity** of colours used **throughout** the book, both for **text and** in diagrams - we feel it helps brighten up the pages !!

T Strang, J Geddes, J Cairns

(May 2014)

* Available for purchase separately.

Contents

1. Write these numbers using **digits** :-

   a   five hundred and seventeen   b   nine hundred and eighty.

2. Write these numbers **in words** :-

   a   93   b   207   c   846   d   940.

3. Write the number that comes :-

   a   just **before** 250   b   100 **after** 630   c   ten **before** 500.

4. In the number **583**, what does the digit :-

   a   **8** stand for   b   **3** stand for   c   **5** stand for ?

5. State whether P, **Q** and R are **right, acute** or **obtuse** angles :-

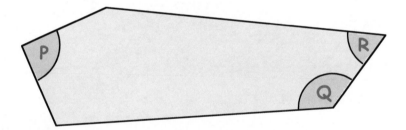

6. How many **right angles** are there in :-

   a   a full turn   b   a half turn ?

7. Is the blue line **parallel** to or **perpendicular** to the **green** line ?

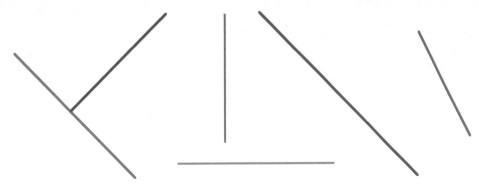

8. Billy is sitting on a wall.

   In real life, is the top of the wall sitting **vertical** or **horizontal** ?

9.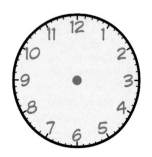

   Give an example of **any** time where the angle between the hour and the minute hand on a clock face is **obtuse**.

10. **Copy** and **work out** :-

   a   46
        + 8
   ───────

   b   9
        + 37
   ───────

   c   65
        + 26
   ───────

   d   59
        + 32
   ───────

   e   365
       + 467
   ───────

   f   84
       + 693
   ───────

   g   483
       + 378
   ───────

   h   295
       + 486
   ───────

11. A cyclist cycled around the 4 sides of a park.

    The diagram shows the lengths of the 4 sides.

    How far did he cycle in **total** ?

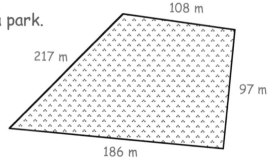

12. Write down the month that comes :-

    a   one month **before** September

    b   two months **after** November.

13. a   What numbers do these stand for :-   (i) VI   (ii) IX ?

    b   Write as Roman numerals :-   (i) 4   (ii) 12.

14. Write each time in 2 ways, (e.g. 8:55 or five to nine) :-

a  b c

15. Write each time in 12 hour form, using **am** or **pm** :-

    a   half past 8 in the evening   b   quarter to eleven in the morning.

16. Work out :-

a	68 - 45	b	458 - 46	c	679 - 358	d	807 - 304
e	42 - 8	f	637 - 79	g	647 - 368	h	903 - 608

17. Find :-

    a 68 – 15   b 625 – 96   c 317 – 148   d 848 – 699.

18. Three band members checked out how much they had in their wallets.

James had £373.

Tom had £195.

John had £308.

    a   How much did they have **altogether** ?

    b   How much **more** did James have than Tom ?

19. a How many **10p** coins can I get for a **£2** coin ?

    b How many **50p** coins can I get for a **£20** note ?

20. a  Pauline got a **£5** note and two **£1** coins as change when she handed over a **£20** note to the hairdresser.

    How much must her haircut have cost Pauline ?

    b What notes and coins might Joe have used to pay **exactly** for his new shoes, which cost **£29** and **75p** ?

21. a Measure the three sides of this triangle in **millimetres**.

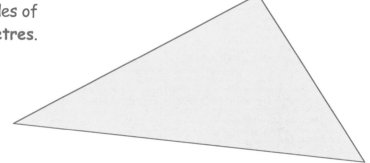

    b Now work out the **perimeter** of the triangle.

22. a Shown is a sketch of a rectangle.

    Make an accurate drawing of the rectangle.

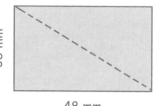

36 mm

48 mm

    b On your drawing, measure the length of the sloping line (dotted).

23.  If you were asked to measure the length of a garden path, would you measure it in **millimetres**, **centimetres** or **metres** ?

24. To make a model of this cuboid, you would need 6 pieces of card, all of them rectangles.

Say what **2-D** shapes you would need to make each of these two shapes :-

a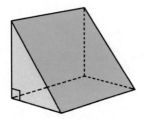

b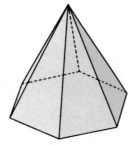

25.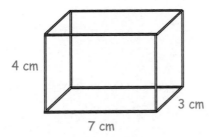

What total length of straws would you need to build this model of a **cuboid** ?

26. Which of these are nets of cubes ?

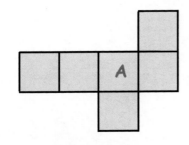 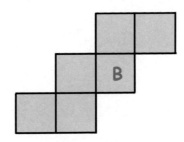 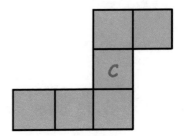

27. Copy and **complete** :-

a   26
      × 3

b   73
      × 2

c   44
      × 5

d   95
      × 4

e   47
      × 10

f   64
      × 8

g   58
      × 4

h   22
      × 8 .

28. What numbers are missing ?

a $5 \times .... = 45$ b $.... \times 4 = 44$ c $10 \times .... = 720$ d $... \times 8 = 160$.

29. **Copy** and **work out** :-

   a $5\overline{)75}$ b $2\overline{)56}$ c $5\overline{)70}$ d $10\overline{)400}$

   e $8\overline{)136}$ f $4\overline{)208}$ g $3\overline{)270}$ h $5\overline{)165}$.

30. **Find** :-

a	126 ÷ 3	b	76 ÷ 2	c	245 ÷ 5	d	176 ÷ 4
e	320 ÷ 10	f	208 ÷ 8	g	140 ÷ 4	h	280 ÷ 8.

31. On a horse racing track, there are 8 **furlongs** in 1 **mile**.

   How many **miles** are there in **120 furlongs** ?

32. **Find** :-

a	37 ÷ 4	b	123 ÷ 5	c	101 ÷ 2	d	152 ÷ 3
e	241 ÷ 5	f	136 ÷ 10	g	234 ÷ 8	h	173 ÷ 4.

33. a What is the day just **before** Wednesday ?

   b Which day comes 2 days **after** Sunday ?

   c Which is the month just **before** January ?

34. a How many days are there in **October** ?

   b How many days are there in a **year** ?

   c How many seconds in a **minute** ?

35. a Write the date 04/05/17 out fully **in words**.

   b Write the date September 2nd 2018 in **number form**.

36. Use **tally marks** to show the numbers :-   a   18   b   33.

37. A class was asked to name their favourite band.

Bluegraz	Girlsown	Calipso	Girlsown	Gameboyz
Gameboyz	Bluegraz	Gameboyz	Calipso	Primevil
Girlsown	Calipso	Bluegraz	Radioham	Girlsown
Primevil	Gameboyz	Gameboyz	Primevil	Gameboyz
Calipso	Primevil	Gameboyz	Calipso	Radioham
Girlsown	Gameboyz	Bluegraz	Gameboyz	Calipso

a   **Copy** and **complete** the tally table.

b   How many said Bluegraz ?

c   How many **more** chose Gameboyz than Radioham ?

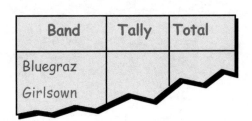

Band	Tally	Total
Bluegraz		
Girlsown		

d   Draw a neat labelled **bar chart** to show all this information.

38. The colour of a batch of cars in a car park was noted at noon.

The table shows the colours :-

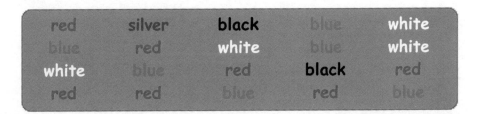

red	silver	black	blue	white
blue	red	white	blue	white
white	blue	red	black	red
red	red	blue	red	blue

a   **Copy** and **complete** the tally table.

b   How many cars were **red** ?

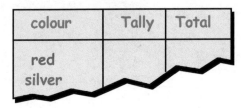

colour	Tally	Total
red		
silver		

c   Draw a **pictograph** to show the information.

Use   [car symbol]   to represent **2 cars**.

Remember to label your diagram.

39. Find **half** of :-   a   16   b   46   c   154.

40. Find a **quarter** of :- a   24   b   64   c   172.

41. What **fraction** does each arrow point to on these number lines ?

42. What **fraction** of each shape is coloured ?

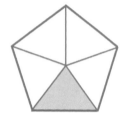  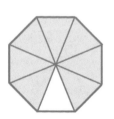 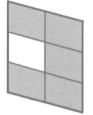

43. Copy and complete to show these **equivalent** fractions :-

a $\frac{1}{2} = \frac{4}{....}$ b $\frac{1}{3} = \frac{2}{...}$ c $\frac{3}{4} = \frac{...}{8}$.

44. Write these fractions in order, **smallest** first :- $\frac{1}{7}, \frac{1}{10}, \frac{1}{3}, \frac{1}{8}, \frac{1}{12}$.

45. Find :-

a $\frac{1}{6} + \frac{4}{6}$ b $\frac{5}{7} - \frac{2}{7}$ c $\frac{1}{3} + \frac{2}{3}$ d $3\frac{4}{5} - \frac{1}{5}$.

46. Find mentally :-

a $7 \times 3 = ...$ b $135 \div 5 = ...$ c $219 + 346 = ...$

d $856 - 314 = ...$ e $4 \times 34 = ...$ f $735 - 123 = ...$

g $176 \div 8 = ...$ h $150 \div 3 = ...$ i $4 \times 75 = ...$

j $144 \div 4 = ...$ k $37 \times 10 = ...$ l $620 \div 10 = ...$

47. For each question here, decide whether to **add**, **subtract**, **multiply** or **divide**, then set down the working neatly and find the answer :-

a   A packet of tea biscuits has **26** biscuits.

How many biscuits in **3** packets ?

b    At a local football match, there were **486** home fans and **237** away fans.

How many fans **in total** attended the football match ?

c   The bill in a restaurant for **4** people, including the tip, came to **£152**.

How much should each person pay ?

d    Of the **840** workers in a factory, **390** of them are men.

How many women must work in the factory ?

48. **Copy** and **complete** these additions and subtractions :-

a   640 ml
   + 270 ml
   _____

b   750 grams
   - 320 grams
   _____

c   2 litres 300 ml
   + 3 litres 400 ml
   _____

49. When Lara baked a cake it weighed 4 kg 620 grams.

Lucy tried to cut it "in half".

Lucy's piece weighed 2 kg 400 grams.

Had Lucy really "cut the cake exactly in half" ?   *Explain.*

Place Value

Understand place value for numbers up to 10 000.

Example :-   In the number **3572**,

	1000 100 10 1
the **3** stands for three thousand	3 0 0 0
the **5** stands for five hundred	5 0 0
the **7** stands for seven tens	7 0
the **2** stands for two units (ones)	2
	3 5 7 2

Three thousand, five hundred and seventy two

3572 ✓

Exercise 1

1. What do the following **digits** stand for in the number 6294 :-

    a   6   b   2   c   9   d   4 ?

2. What does the **4** stand for in each of these numbers :-

    a   4392   b   6540   c   3694   d   7488 ?

3. Write out the following numbers fully **in words** :-

    a   1720   b   3586   c   2908   d   8009

    e   931   f   6340   g   5087   h   9876.

4. Write the following numbers **using digits** :-

    a   four hundred and forty four   b   nine hundred and six

    c   three thousand one hundred and seventy two

    d   five thousand two hundred and seven

    e   eight thousand four hundred and sixty six

    f   seven thousand seven hundred

    g   eight thousand three hundred and ninety nine

    h   nine thousand and fifty.

I'm only four hundred and forty four years old today.

5. Write down the number that is :-

    a   10 more than 680   b   400 more than 800

    c   40 less than 950   d   200 less than 1300

    e   500 more than 3800   f   1000 less than 7300

    g   1000 more than 6500   h   1000 less than 9500

    i   3200 less than 9200   j   2100 less than 7100.

6. Put the following numbers in order, **smallest first** :-

    a   380, 402, 399, 400, 413, 335, 381, 410, 397.

    b   3054, 3095, 2985, 2895, 3009, 3100, 2899, 3002.

    c   8243, 8432, 8234, 8300, 8200, 8400, 8355, 8249.

7. What numbers do **A, B, C,** .... stand for in these scales ?

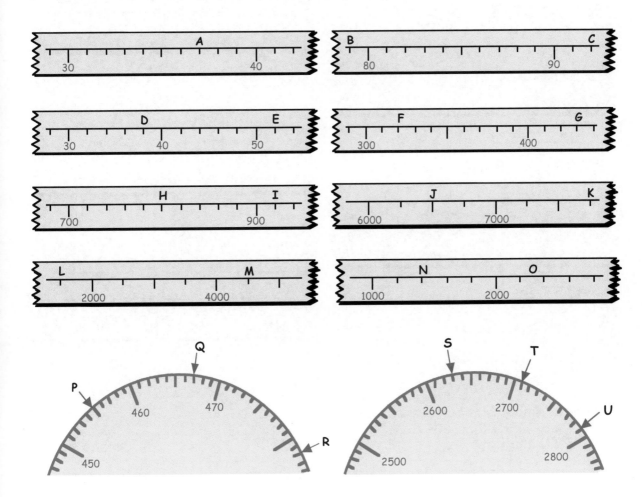

8. What are the readings on these thermometers ?

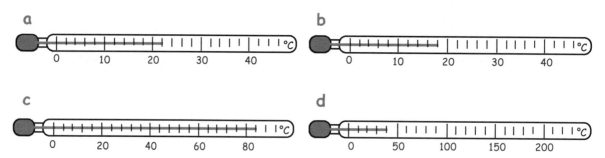

a

b

c

d

9. Write down the numbers that are represented by each letter :-

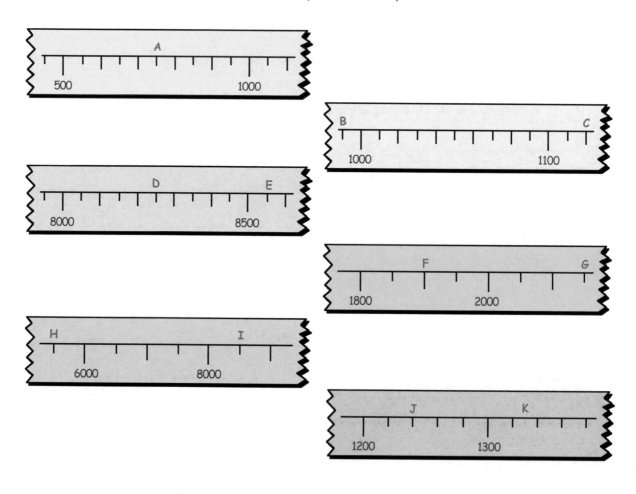

10. What number lies **half way** between :-

    a   200 and 260   b   800 and 1200   c   4000 and 4600

    d   3000 and 7000   e   5500 and 6500   f   2000 and 8000 ?

Going up in 6's, 7's, 9's, 25's and 1000's

Recognise patterns of numbers going up in 6's, 7's, 9's, 25's and 1000's.

You should already be able to recognise patterns which go up in multiples of 2, 3, 4, 5, 8, 10, 50 and 100. The following exercise will remind you of that.

Look at these patterns :-

a	0,	6,	12,	18,	....	Numbers go up in **6's**. Next number **24**
b	0,	7,	14,	21,	....	Numbers go up in **7's**. Next number **28**
c	0,	9,	18,	27,	....	Numbers go up in **9's**. Next number **36**
d	0,	25,	50,	75,	....	Numbers go up in **25's**. Next number **100**
e	0,	1000,	2000,		....	Numbers go up in **1000's**. Next number **3000**

You will find out more about going up in 6's, 7's and 9's later in the book

Exercise 2

1. Write down the **next 2 numbers** in each of these patterns :-

    a 40, 42, 44, 46, ...   b 86, 83, 80, 77, ...

    c 176, 180, 184, ...   d 235, 240, 245, ...

    e 40, 48, 56, 64, ...   f 400, 390, 380, 370, ...

    g 660, 560, 460, ...   h 18, 24, 30, 36, ...

    i 49, 42, 35, 28, ...   j 27, 36, 45, 54, ...

    k 250, 225, 200, 175, ...   l 2500, 3500, 4500, ...

2. Find the missing numbers :-

    a 12, 18, ... 30, ...   b 14, 21, ... 35, ...

    c 63, 54, ..., ..., 27   d 175, ..., 225, ..., 275

    e 10000, ..., 8000, ..., 6000   f 70, ..., 90, ..., 110

    g 1120, 1110, ..., ..., 1080   h 3456, ..., 5456, ..., 7456.

Roman Numerals - The History

Long before our counting system using 1, 2, 3, 4, 5 ....
came into being, there were lots of other ways of counting.

The **Roman Empire** was based in and around Italy just over 2000 years ago, and they were the most important race for nearly 500 years.

They devised a counting system based on a series
of **strokes**, which (*some believe*) were based on
the fingers of the two hands.

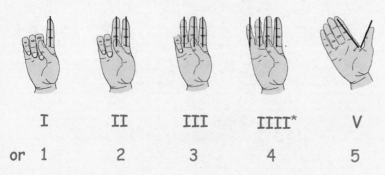

I	II	III	IIII*	V
or 1	2	3	4	5

IIII* is in fact **not** correct.
We use IV or (1 before 5) for 4.

Exercise 3

1. What number do you think a Roman is showing when
   he holds his two hands like this ?

2. What numbers do you think these hands are showing ?

a   b   c   d

3. So far, we have seen that the Romans wrote the numbers 1 to 5 like this :-

   I = **1**,   II = **2**,   III = **3**,   IV = **4** and   V = **5**.

   Just as **4** is shown as **IV** (*1 before 5*), how would you write **6** in Roman terms ?

4. Use the hands from Question **2** to write the numbers 7 - 10 as Roman symbols.

5. Try to find out what the Roman symbol for 0 was ?

Roman Numbers

Be able to write 1 to 50 in Roman Symbol form.

Rather than use long strings of I's and V's to represent numbers, the Romans came up with a few more letters to help cut down on the number of strokes needed.

Like our modern number system, the Romans based theirs on the number 10.

Question - Can you think why 10 was used ?

Instead of using V V to stand for **10**, the Romans used X.

The numbers now run as :-

> I, II, III, IV, V, VI, VII, VIII, IX*, X.

The Romans had **no** symbol to stand for **Zero (0)**.

IX* is used instead of VIIII.
IX means (1 before 10 = 9).

Exercise 4

1. If **10** is shown as X, what do you think **11** will be represented by ?

2. Try to think of the Roman form of these numbers :-

   a 12   b 13   c 14 (not XIIII)   d 15 (not XIIIII).

3. a **Explain** why you think the number 15 should be shown as XV.

   b Now **explain** why you think the number 14 will be shown as XIV.

4. If **15** is shown as XV, what do you think **16** will be represented by ?

5. Try to think of the Roman form of these numbers :-

   a 17   b 18   c 19 (not XVIIII)   d 20.

6. Here are a couple of other numbers to help :- **27** = XXVII, **35** = XXXV.

   Now try to write all the numbers from 21 to 50 in Roman form.

Roman Numbers from 35 to 100

Be able to write 1 to 100 in Roman Symbol form.

The number **50** is not represented by XXXXX.

Neither is the number **40** shown as XXXX.

Just as V and X were introduced to save long strings of symbols, a new letter (L) is introduced to stand for **50**.

> The Romans made a rule :- You could not have **four** or more of the same symbols (I, V, X or L) together.

This means that **40** is not XXXX It is in fact XL. Can you explain why ?

Can you explain why :-   **45 = XLV**,   **39 = XXXIX**   **49 = XLIX** ?

7. Now go back over the Roman numbers you wrote for **35** to **50** and write them correctly this time using the new rules given above.

8. Here are a couple of other numbers to help :- 66 = LXVI, 87 = LXXXVII.

   Now try to write all the numbers from 51 to 90 in Roman form.

> The next letter the Romans introduced was the letter C.   C stands for 100.
>
> Explain why :-   **70 = LXX**,   **89 = LXXXIX**   **95 = XCV** .

9. Try to write all the numbers from I to C.

10. A bit of fun. Imagine today that we still used Roman numbers in our everyday life instead of 1, 2, 3, 4, 5, ...

    • You could say there are **VI** members in your family.

    • Your telephone number might be **VIII VII II IV VI IX I**.

    • A pair of new trainers cost £**XXXV** and **XC** pence.

   Make up a story with as many number facts as you can think of, but only use Roman Numerals in your story. Display the best stories.

1. Write out the number 7385 fully in words.

2. Write these numbers using digits :-

    a   three thousand seven hundred and four   b   nine thousand and eleven.

3. Rearrange the numbers given below in order, starting with the largest :-

    8029   9080   9001   8892   9009   9010.

4. a   What numbers are represented by P, Q, R and S on the given scales ?

       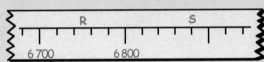

    b   What is the reading on this thermometer ?

    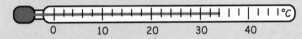

5. What number lies halfway between :-

    a   4000 and 8000   b   5500 and 9500 ?

6. Write down the number that is :-

    a   2000 more than 6900   b   500 less than 9100.

7. Write down the next two numbers each time :-

    a   250, 255, 260, ..., ...   b   730, 720, 710, ..., ...

    c   30, 36, 42, ..., ...   d   70, 63, 56, ..., ...

    e   7200, 7100, 7000, ..., ...   f   7200, 6200, 5200, ..., ...

8. What numbers are missing ?

    a   7, ..., 21, 28, ...   b   9 ...., 27, 36, ...

    c   8150, ..., ..., 8450, 8550   d   9250, 9225, ..., 9175, ...

9. a   Change to number form :-   (i) XVI   (ii) LXXIX   (iii) XCV.

    b   Change to Roman form :-   (i) 19   (ii) 44   (iii) 79.

Lines of Symmetry

Recognise if a shape has lines of symmetry.

A shape has a **line of symmetry** if, when you fold the shape over the line, the 2 halves **exactly** match.

This **triangle** has a **(green)** line of symmetry .

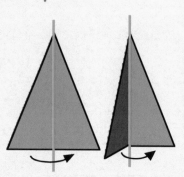

Examples :-

These shapes are symmetrical.

Some shapes have more than 1 line of symmetry.

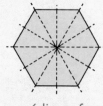

1 line of symmetry

2 lines of symmetry

6 lines of symmetry

Exercise 1   (You will need a ruler and tracing paper).

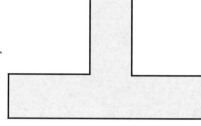

1. a   Trace this shape neatly.

   b   Either cut it out and fold it (or just fold it).

   c   Check it has 1 line of symmetry.

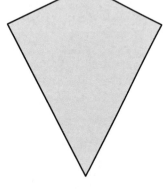

2.   Copy or trace the shape shown and by folding, check whether it has a line of symmetry or not.

   a   Name the shape.

   b   State how many lines of symmetry it has.

3. Trace each of the following shapes and by folding, check whether the shape has a line of symmetry or not.

    (Mark any lines of symmetry **dotted** or in **colour**).

    a 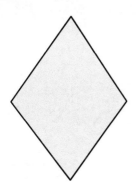   b 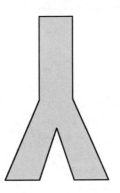   c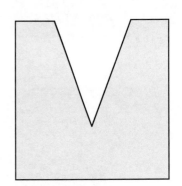

Some shapes have more than 1 line of symmetry.

Can you see that this **hexagon** has 6 ?

They are shown in red.

Try tracing or drawing the hexagon and check the 6 lines over which you can fold it neatly.

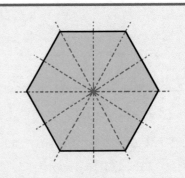

4. Make a neat tracing of each of the following shapes.

    Use a coloured pencil to show all the lines of symmetry, (dotted).

    Write down beside each shape how many lines of symmetry it has.

    a 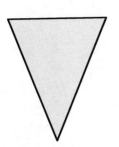   b 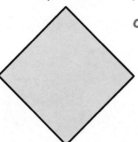   c 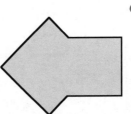   d

    e 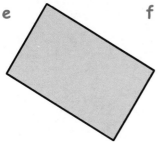   f    g    h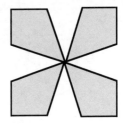

4.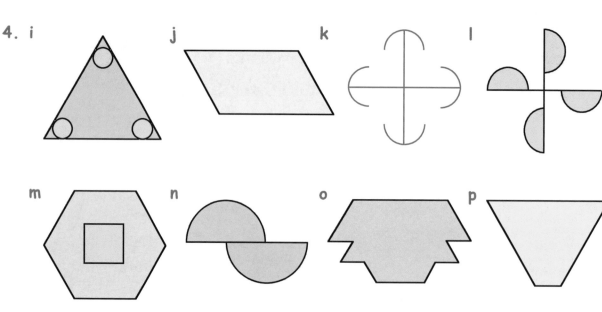

   i   j   k   l

   m   n   o   p

5. a   Trace the **equilateral** triangle shown.

    b   Fold it to check how many
        lines of symmetry it has.

    c   Mark the lines of symmetry
        and state how many there are.

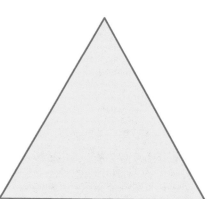

6. Of the following shapes, **six** of them have **NO** lines of symmetry.

  (i)   Find the 6 shapes with no lines of symmetry.

  (ii)   State how many lines of symmetry each of the other shapes has.

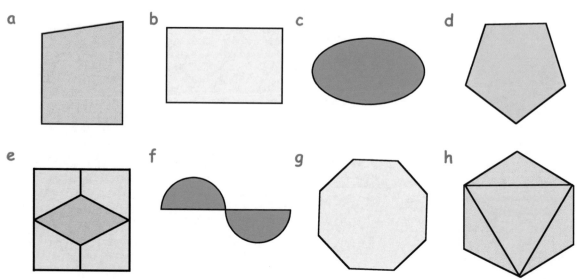

   a   b   c   d

   e   f   g   h

6.

i   j   k   l

m   n   o   p

q   r   s   t

u   v   w   x

7. Draw and colour **any** shape with the following number of
    lines of symmetry :-

    a 3   b 5   c 6   d 10.

8. Look at the diagram in question **6x.**

    Write down a time on a clock face that **does** have a line of symmetry.

9. Can 3-D shapes have symmetry ? **Discuss.**

Creating a Symmetrical Shape

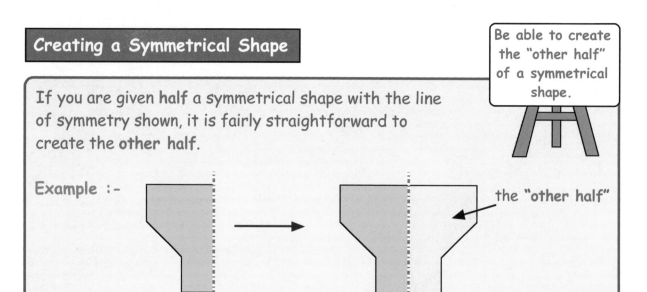

If you are given **half** a symmetrical shape with the line of symmetry shown, it is fairly straightforward to create the **other half**.

Example :-

the "other half"

Exercise 2

1. a **Trace** or **copy** this shape into your notebook, or onto a piece of paper.

   b Now draw and shade/colour the other half so that the **red** dotted line is a line of symmetry.

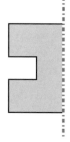

2. Repeat question 1 for this shape.

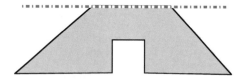

3. **Trace** or **copy** each of the following shapes, then complete each shape so that the **red** dotted line is a line of symmetry.

a

b

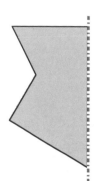

c

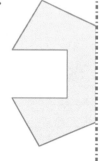

3.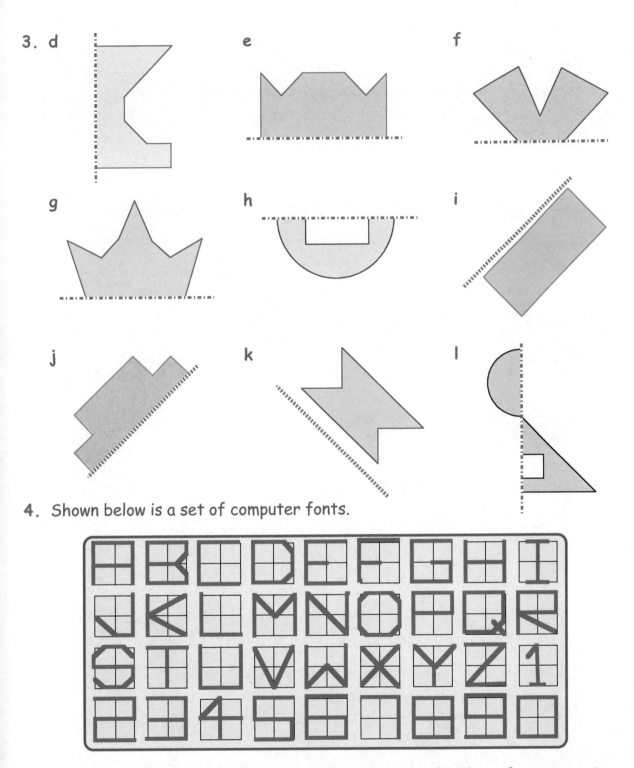

4. Shown below is a set of computer fonts.

a   Which of the above letters/numbers have **exactly** 1 line of symmetry ?

b   Which of them have **two** lines of symmetry ?

c   Which have **NO** lines of symmetry ?

d   Which have **more** than **two** lines of symmetry ?

5. Neatly, write out your name on squared paper using the above set of fonts.

The 3 Я's

Revisit - Review - Revise

1. Define, in your own words, what is meant by saying that a shape has a line of symmetry.

2. How many lines of symmetry do each of the following shapes have ?

   a    b 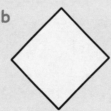   c 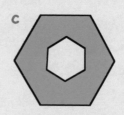   d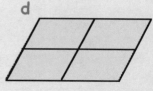

   e 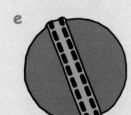   f 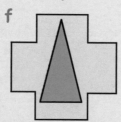   g    h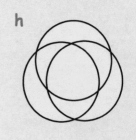

3. Trace or copy these shapes NEATLY onto squared paper.

   a 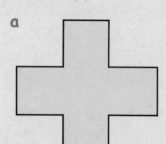   b 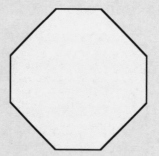   c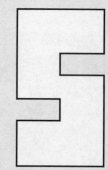

Mark in co our ALL the lines of symmetry you can find.

4. Trace or copy the following shapes neatly and draw in the other half so the red dotted lines are lines of symmetry.

   a 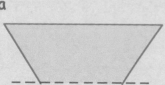   b    c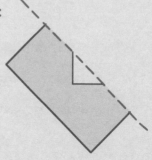

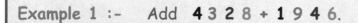

Chapter 3

Whole Numbers 2

Add/Subtract Numbers with up to 4 Digits

> Be able to add
> & subtract
> numbers with up
> to 4 digits.

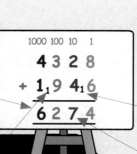

Example 1 :-   Add **4 3 2 8 + 1 9 4 6**.

Set down and work
out as before :-
Start with the 1's

$$4\,3\,2\,8 + 1\,9\,4\,6 = 6\,2\,7\,4$$

1 + 1 + 4 = 6
= 6 thousand

```
1000 100 10  1
   4 3 2 8
+  1,9 4,6
   6 2 7 4
```

6 + 8 = 14
= 4 units (1's)
carry 1 (ten)

1 + 4 + 2 = 7
= 7 tens
no carry

9 + 3 = 12
= 2 hundreds
carry 1
(thousand)

> * Remember to line
> up the numbers

> * Remember to add the
> numbers you have carried

Example 2 :-   Work out **9 2 4 6 - 2 7 5 9**.

Your teacher will explain this.

$$9\,2\,4\,6 - 2\,7\,5\,9 = 6\,4\,8\,7$$

```
1000 100 10  1
  8  1  3  1
  9  2  4  6
-  2  7  5  9
   6  4  8  7
```

* Note :-
   The answer can be checked by adding.
      6487 + 2759 = 9246. ✓

Exercise 1   *Check your answers to subtractions by adding as in the *Note above.*

1. Copy each example and work out the answer :-

a	352 + 168	b	469 + 357	c	386 + 566	d	978 + 213
e	626 − 386	f	5003 + 3087	g	3456 + 5678	h	7374 − 5895

1.　i　3000　　　　j　　7777　　　k　　6052　　　l　　10 000
　　　　– 893　　　　　　+ 1999　　　　　– 3463　　　　　– 8409

　　m　5389 + 364　　n　2345 + 6666　　o　8527 – 5521　　p　8000 – 374

　　q　5802 + 3299　　r　7006 – 2967　　s　10 000 – 7391　　t　8429 + 1571.

2.　There were 2872 Exeter supporters and 4188 Torquay
　　supporters at the local derby match.

　　a　How many supporters were there **altogether** ?

　　b　How many **more** Torquay than Exeter supporters were there ?

3.　From 9 pm until midnight a train travels 637 kilometres.

　　From midnight until 1 am it travels 199 kilometres.

　　How far has the train travelled **in total** ?

4.　　　A delivery man earned £9290 last year.

　　　　　　This year his pay **dropped** by £745.

　　　　　　What was his salary this year ?

5.　The local newspaper prints 10 000 copies per week.

　　The paper sold 8645 copies last week.

　　How many copies were **not** sold ?

6.　　　A football manager was fined £3250 for shouting
　　　　　　at a referee, **plus** £1950 court hearing costs.

　　　　　　How much in total did the manager have to pay ?

7.　Harry bought 3250 bricks to build a wall.

　　When he had finished, he found he had 280 bricks **left over**.

　　How many bricks had Harry used to build the wall ?

Add/Subtract Whole Numbers mentally

Be able to add & subtract numbers with up to 4 digits mentally.

There are **quick ways** of adding and subtracting numbers.

Example 1 :-   To add **390** and **540**,

you could add :-		you could add :-
390 + 500 = 890,	**OR**	400 + 540 = 940,
then **add** 40 = 930		then **subtract** 10 = 930

Example 2 :-   What is **5600 – 2900** ?

You could subtract :-		You could subtract :-
5600 – 2000 = 3600,	**OR**	5600 – 3000 = 2600,
then **subtract** 900 = 2700		then **add** 100 = 2700

*Discuss these and other methods.

Exercise 2   Try to do this exercise **mentally**.

1.   Write down the answers to :-

a	48 + 35	b	53 + 29	c	69 + 37	d	17 + 98
e	85 + 55	f	76 + 75	g	126 + 58	h	80 + 79
i	350 + 290	j	410 + 390	k	460 + 750	l	830 + 990
m	5600 + 3500	n	3800 + 4200	o	7800 + 1400	p	2850 + 7150.

2.   Write down the answers to :-

a	63 – 51	b	74 – 39	c	66 – 38	d	41 – 16
e	90 – 35	f	80 – 25	g	100 – 43	h	180 – 49
i	360 – 290	j	780 – 440	k	470 – 190	l	540 – 180
m	2900 – 880	n	4400 – 2600	o	6600 – 3700	p	10 000 – 1100.

3. Work out :-

   a   360 + 770   b   1630 – 590   c   5450 + 3900   d   6740 – 4350

   e   7650 + 1670   f   8880 – 2280   g   1530 + 4290   h   9780 – 8790.

4. a   A train with 160 passengers stops at a station.

   At the station, 38 people get on the train.

   How many are there now on the train ?

   b    The garage charged Mr Grant £199 for parts and
       £104 for labour.

       How much was Mr Grant's **total** garage bill ?

   c   Alex earns £2500 per month and Drew earns £1900.

       (i)   How much do they earn **altogether** ?

       (ii) How much **more** does Alex earn than Drew ?

5. a   Of the 3510 miles from Manchester to
       Dubai, a plane had flown 2925 miles.

       How much **further** had it to travel ?

   b    Declan won £1300 on a scratch card.

       He bought a new laptop for £890.

       How much had Declan left ?

   c   Sandra has 6400 stamps in her collection.

       Four thousand five hundred of them are British.

       How many stamps in her collection are **not** British ?

   d   Last year, Barry sent 4520 text messages.

       This year he sent 4370 messages.

       (i)   How many text messages did Barry send **in total** ?

       (ii) How many **more** messages did he send last year ?

Rounding to the nearest 10

Be able to round a whole number to the nearest 10.

Shown is a number line :-

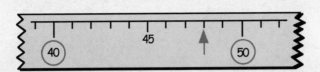

The arrow points to the number **48**.

- Notice that **48** lies between **40** and **50**.

- Can you see that **48** is closer to **50** than **40** ?

We say that, " **48**, rounded to **the nearest 10**, is **50**."

> **Rule** If the last digit is a 0, 1, 2, 3, 4 - **ROUND DOWN**
>
> If the last digit is a 5, 6, 7, 8, 9 - **ROUND UP**

Exercise 3

1. Look at this number line.

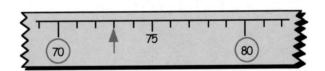

   Copy the following and complete :-

   - **73** lies between **70** and .....

   - **73** is closer to ..... than .....

   - **73** rounds to ..... (*to the nearest 10*).

2. **Copy** and complete :-

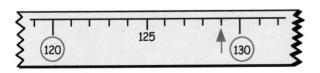

   - **129** lies between **120** and ...

   - **129** is closer to ..... than ...

   - **129** rounds to ... (*to the nearest 10*).

3. **Copy** and complete :-
- 24 lies between **20** and .....
- 24 is closer to ... than .....
- 24 rounds to .... (*to the nearest 10*).

4. Imagine the following numbers and decide what each one rounds to, (*to the nearest 10*). **Copy** and **complete** :-

a   **87** lies between 80 and .....   It is closer to .....

b   **133** lies between ..... and 140   It is closer to .....

c   **458** lies between 450 and .....   It is closer to .....

d   **902** lies between 900 and .....   It is closer to .....

A short way of writing   **"68 rounds to 70 to the nearest 10"**

is to simply write   **68 —› 70**

If a number ends in a **5**, we round up - **75 —› 80** (*not 70*).

---

5. **Copy** each of the following and round, (*to the nearest 10*) :-

a   37 —› ......   b   71 —›   c   18 —› ......   d   63 —› ......

e   159 —› ......   f   141 —› ......   g   316 —› ......   h   534 —› ......

i   45 —› ......   j   405 —› ......   k   703 —›   l   6125 —› ......

6. a   The height of this pot is **33** centimetres.
   Round this to the nearest **10** cm.

b      My jet to Tenerife reached **506** miles per hour.
   Round this to the nearest **10** miles per hour.

c   A tennis professional earns **£1854** per month.
   Round this to the nearest **£10**.

Rounding to the nearest 100 and 1000

To round to the nearest **100**   look at the **tens** digit :-

- if it is a 0, 1, 2, 3 or 4 -   leave the 100's digit as it is.
- if it is a 5, 6, 7, 8 or 9 -   round the 100's digit **UP** by one.

Example :-   476 —> 500

To round to the nearest **1000**   look at the **hundreds** digit :-

- if it is a 0, 1, 2, 3 or 4 -   leave the 1000's digit as it is.
- if it is a 5, 6, 7, 8 or 9 -   round the 1000's digit **UP** by one.

Example :-   1729 —> 1700

Extension Example :-   Round 34 700 to the nearest thousand.

As the hundreds digit is 7, the 1000's go up !

34 700 —> 35 000

Exercise 4

1. *Revision* Round to the **nearest 10** :-

a	68	b	23	c	76	d	85
e	7	f	434	g	486	h	691
i	16	j	805	k	937	l	899
m	7851	n	4805	o	8999	p	7358.

2. Round to the **nearest 100** :-

a	631	b	873	c	627	d	759
e	452	f	619	g	2549	h	4081
i	6609	j	5993	k	3255	l	6764
m	3270	n	8792	o	9020	p	5658.

3. Round to the **nearest 1000** :-

a	1600	b	5300	c	8940	d	9870
e	2397	f	1504	g	951	h	3375
i	5920	j	3492	k	4872	l	6800
m	7493	n	9709	o	3400	p	4700.

4. An ice hockey match in the Winter Olympic Games had an attendance of 7652.

Round this figure to the nearest :-

a   10   b   100   c   1000.

5.

9985 copies of the local newspaper were sold last week.

Round this figure to the nearest :-

a   10   b   100   c   1000.

6. A car is on sale at the village garage for £9738.

Round this amount to the nearest :-

a   £10   b   £100   c   £1000.

7.

4619 people voted in the recent council by-election.

Round this figure to the nearest :-

a   10   b   100   c   1000.

8. A survey showed that in one evening, 7864 vehicles passed over the *Golden Gate Bridge* in San Francisco.

Round this figure to the nearest :-

a   10   b   100   c   1000.

Using Rounding to Estimate Answers

Be able to estimate an answer to a question using rounding.

It is possible to "**MENTALLY**" estimate the answer to a question by rounding the numbers to "**1 figure**" accuracy first.

Example 1 :-

> 51 + 78
> is approximately
> 50 + 80
> ≈ 130

Example 2 :-

> 792 – 323
> is approximately
> 800 – 300
> ≈ 500

"≈" **means** approximately equal to.

Exercise 5

1. Round each number to **1 figure accuracy**, then give an *estimate* to :-

   a   18 + 61   b   41 + 57   c   72 – 56   d   68 + 23

   e   91 – 19   f   285 + 119   g   708 – 169   h   137 + 917

   i   456 + 274   j   890 - 678   k   1811 + 518   l   3822 – 829.

2. a   Denis has 291 Jinju cards, Frank has 87.

   Approximately, how many do they have in total ?

   b   Cheryl has saved £423. Heather has saved £572.

   Approximately, how much have they saved in total ?

   c   Calculate, approximately, the **total** distance around the square shown.

Yoshi   Tishu

48 cm

3. Give an approximate answer to each of the following :-

   a   66 – 28   b   88 – 21   c   417 – 98   d   807 – 180

   e   915 – 777   f   888 – 326   g   2841 – 1100   h   5281 – 2810.

4. a   Of the 2310 bananas delivered to a supermarket, 198 of them were bad.

   Approximately how many of the bananas were ok to eat ?

   b   *Estimate* the answer to :-   199 + 299 + 399 + 499.

The 3 Я's

Revisit - Review - Revise

1. Set down and then work out :-

   a   5264
        + 2927

   b   6327 - 1851

   c   7896
        + 999

   d   10 000
        - 2947

2. A train carried 1479 passengers from Liverpool to London.

   On the return journey there were 1592 passengers.

   What was the total number of passengers for both trips ?

3. Henry raised £3216 for charity. Sebastian raised £5197.

   How much **more** money did Sebastian raise than Henry ?

4. Do the following **mentally** (*no working should be seen*) :-

   a   59 + 77   b   138 + 99   c   2700 + 3300   d   83 - 29

   e   1700 - 250   f   10 000 - 5700   g   7888 + 1200   h   5000 - 75.

5. Round to the :-

   a   nearest 10 :-   (i)   73   (ii)   486   (iii)   575

   b   nearest 100 :-   (i)   347   (ii)   2762   (iii)   8611

   c   nearest 1000 :-   (i)   1628   (ii)   5099   (iii)   10 500.

6. There were 3995 spectators at Wimbledon on day one.

   Round this number to the nearest :- a 10   b 100   c 1000.

7.

   A baker has a total of 813 apples.

   He uses 296 of them to make apple pies.

   The rest he uses to make apple crumbles.

   Estimate how many apples are for crumbles.

   Do **not** give the exact answer.

Chapter 4

| 12 Hour & Calendar Time | Revision

Time 1

Be able to read and write 12 hour and calendar times.

Exercise 1 *You may wish to do this exercise orally.*

1. Write down each of the following times using **am** and **pm** :-

    a   half past nine in the evening   b   ten to eleven at night

    c   quarter to four in the afternoon   d   fifteen minutes after midnight

    e   seven minutes before midnight   f   twenty to seven in the morning.

2. Write each of these times using **am** and **pm** :-

    a   Kyle went swimming from five to ten in the
        morning until ten past one in the afternoon.

    b   Write all the times of the day your school bell rings.

3. a   Write down the months of the year
        in reverse !   (December, Nov.....).

    b   Write down how many days there
        are in each month.

    > 30 days has September, April,
    > June and November.
    > All the rest have 31, except
    > February which has 28 days clear
    > and 29 in each leap year.

4. Write each date below using **6 digits** :-

    a   fourteenth of May 2016   b   tenth of September 2008

    c   today   d   your birthday.

5. Write down the **day and date** :-

    a   2 days before Tue 18th April   b   a week after Wed 10th Sept

    c   a day after Saturday 30th May   d   5 days before Mon 4th October

    e   a week before Sun 5th April   f   3 weeks before Thu 28th Jan.

12 & 24 Hour Time

Be able to read
and write time
using 12 and 24
hour clock.

We usually think of the time of day in terms of midnight to noon, (ante-meridian - morning) and noon to midnight, (post- meridian - after noon/night), but pilots and sailors need a system that causes no confusion.

Imagine turning up for your plane to Tenerife at 7.00 (**pm**) to find it had flown away at 7.00 (**am**) and you missed your holiday !

The 24 hour Clock

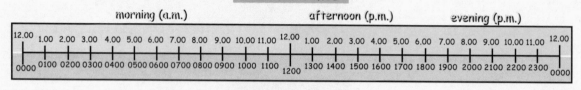

12 hour times

morning (a.m.)   afternoon (p.m.)   evening (p.m.)

12.00 1.00 2.00 3.00 4.00 5.00 6.00 7.00 8.00 9.00 10.00 11.00 12.00 1.00 2.00 3.00 4.00 5.00 6.00 7.00 8.00 9.00 10.00 11.00 12.00
0000 0100 0200 0300 0400 0500 0600 0700 0800 0900 1000 1100 1200 1300 1400 1500 1600 1700 1800 1900 2000 2100 2200 2300 0000

24 hour times

Example :-   Can you see that morning times in 24 hour format stay almost the same ?

6.00 am	becomes	0600 hrs
8.45 am	becomes	0845 hrs
11.20 am	becomes	1120 hrs

But for afternoon and evening times, you always **add on 12 hours** :-

3.00 pm	becomes	1500 hrs	(*3 hours past 12.00 o'clock*)
6.15 pm	becomes	1815 hrs	(6.15 + 12.00)
10.40 pm	becomes	2240 hrs	(10.40 + 12.00)

Exercise 2

1. Change the following 12 hour clock times to **24 hour clock times** :-
    (*e.g. 7.10 am —> 0710*)

    a   8.40 am   b   3.55 am   c   5.00 am

    d   3.30 pm   e   2.15 pm   f   8.00 pm

1. **g** 5.45 am   **h** 10.20 pm   **i** 4.35 am

    j 9.55 am   **k** noon   **l** 12.20 am

    m 12.20 pm   **n** 9.30 pm   **o** 7.55 am

    p 11.30 pm   **q** 11.32 pm   **r** 7.36 am

    s 10.58 pm   **t** 11.19 am   **u** 8.48 pm

    v 2.01 am   **w** 2.01 pm   **x** midnight.

2. When changing 12 hour pm times -> 24 hour clock

         -> you needed to **add on** 12.

    Suggest how you might change from 24 hour -> 12 hour **pm** clock times.

3. Change the following 24 hour clock times to **12 hour clock times** :-
(*remember am and pm*)

    a 0330   **b** 1150   **c** 0910

    d 1535   **e** 1750   **f** 2235

    g 0230   **h** 1835   **i** 2040

    j 1902   **k** 1200   **l** 0750

    m 0445   **n** 1625   **o** 2325

    p 2205   **q** 0050   **r** 0305

    s 1135   **t** 1940   **u** 2348.

4. Write each of these times in 12 hour clock **and** in 24 hour clock time :-

    a   **b**   **c**

      **8:05**

     during the night   football match
kicked off   ready to leave for
school

4.
d	e	f
		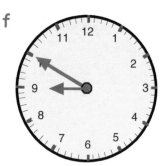
alarm clock goes off	home from school	thinking about bed

5. **a** The US Airways plane left New York at 9.50 pm
       and touched down at Gatwick at 5.35 am.

       Write these times in 24 hour form.

    b  One evening in April, the sun set at 2115
       and rose the following morning at 0525.

       Write these times in 12 hour form.

    c The school disco started at half past six and
       finished at quarter to nine.

       Write these times in 12 **and** 24 hour time.

6. Katie had three appointments in her notebook.

    She **arrived** at the hospital at 9.20 am, the opticians
    at quarter to one and her lawyer at 4.25 pm.

    a For each appointment, write whether
       she was on time or she was late.

    b How many minutes late or early was she for each appointment ?

7. Write each of these times in 12 hour time **and** in 24 hour time :-

    a breakfast   **b** lunch at the weekend

    c Sunday dinner   **d** bedtime on a school night

    e bedtime at the weekend   **f** wake up time on a Sunday.

Simple Time Intervals

Be able to calculate simple time intervals.

Counting on :- The easiest way of finding how long something lasts is by "counting on".

Example :- A TV show starts at 7.45 pm and ends at 8.25 pm. How long did it last ?

Answer :-

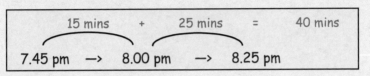

| 15 mins | + | 25 mins | = | 40 mins |

7.45 pm —> 8.00 pm —> 8.25 pm

Exercise 3

1. a How many **hours** is it from **2 o'clock** to **5 o'clock** ?
       (*Hint - "count on" from 2 up to 5*).

    b How many **hours** is it from **3 o'clock** to **8 o'clock** ?

    c How many **hours** is it from **1500 hours** to **1900 hours** ?

    d How many **hours** is it from **half past 3** to **half past 5** ?

    e How many **hours** is it from **quarter past 2** to **quarter past 7** ?

    f How many **hours** is it from **6:15 am** to **11:15 am** ?

    g How many **hours** is it from **1410** to **1810** ?

2. Use the method shown above to find how many **minutes** there are between :-

    a 2:45 pm and 3:05 pm   b 4:50 am and 5:25 am

    c 1:40 pm and 2:20 pm   d 7:45 am and 8:25 am

    e 10:35 pm and 11:25 pm   f 1:30 am and 2:15 am

    g 14:50 and 15:15   h 17:35 and 18:05

    i 1335 and 1420   j 1655 and 1745

    k 2210 and 2305   l 1956 and 2037.

3. The bus station clock is shown.

a My bus leaves at **quarter to two**.

How many **minutes** until my bus leaves ?

b Jack's bus leaves in **45 minutes** time.

At what time does his bus leave ?

c The bus to town leaves in **1 hour and 10 minutes** time.

At what time does the bus leave ?

4. The times of cartoons on an animated TV channel are shown below.

	Cartoon A	Cartoon B	Cartoon C	Cartoon D	Cartoon E
Start Time	9.40 am	10.45 am	11.35 am	12.35 pm	1.30 pm
Show lasted	20 mins	30 mins	45 mins	55 mins	1 hr 10 mins

Write down the times each cartoon finishes.

5. Shown is part of the bus timetable from Malton to Highrose.

	Malton ➤ Lugton ➤ Blythe ➤ Fenton ➤ Highrose				
Early Bus	7.45 am	8.00 am	8.35 am	9.15 am	10.00 am
Late Bus	12.05 pm	12.20 pm			2.20 pm

a How long does the early bus take to travel from :–

(i) Malton to Lugton   (ii) Blythe to Fenton

(iii) Malton to Highrose ?

b Assuming that the late bus travels at the same speed as the early bus, when would it be expected to arrive at :–

(i) Blythe   (*Hint ! Notice how long the early bus takes from Lugton to Blythe*).

(ii) Fenton ?

c On a Sunday, the buses leave Malton at 8.25 am and 1 pm.

Write out a new timetable for Sunday.

Calendar and Longer Time Intervals

Be able to interpret and use a calendar.

You should know that there are :-

12 months in a year

365 days in a year.

Leap years have 366. They occur every 4 years.

Exercise 4

| April 2014 |
| Su Mo Tu We Th Fr Sa |

Su	Mo	Tu	We	Th	Fr	Sa
		1	2	3	4	5
6	7	8	9	10	11	12
13	14	15	16	17	18	19
20	21	22	23	24	25	26
27	28	29	30			

Calendar tab for Apr 2014

1. a   What is the **1st** month of the year ?

    b   What is the **last** month of the year ?

    c   Which month comes just **after** July ?

    d   Which month comes just **before** May ?

    e   Write down all 12 months in the correct order.

2. How many days are there in the month of :-

    a   January   b   February   c   April   d   December ?

3. How many months are there in :-

    a   2 years   b   4 years   c   8 years   d   a decade ?
    (ten years)

4. How many days are there in :-

    a   2 years   b   3 years   c   4 years   d   10 years ?

5. *Including* both dates, how many days are there from :-

    a   8th of May and 30th of May   b   21st April and 3rd of May

    c   18/08/14 and 30/08/14   d   11/04/15 and 11/05/15

    e   July 1st to August 2nd   f   4th December to New Years day

    g   8th May to 10th June   h   Halloween to Guy Fawkes day ?

The 3 Я's

Revisit - Review - Revise

1. Change these times to **24 hour format** :-

   a 7.50 am   b 4.05 pm   c 25 to midnight

   d Noon   e half past midnight   f 20 to 11 at night.

2. Write the following in **12 hour format** :-   (*remember to use am or pm*)

   a 0605   b 1550   c 1157   d 2357

   e 1933   f 1700   g 0010   h 1112.

3. How many **minutes** are there between :-

   a 6 pm and 10 pm   b 2:50 pm and 3:15 pm

   c 1845 and 1925   d 0910 an 1045 ?

4. A cruise ship spends its day sailing a circular route in Lake Arness.

   The times below are of the first two sailings from the jetty.

	Jetty	Falcon Point	Rose Harbour	Stove Castle	Wallace Mount	Floral Gardens	Jetty
1st Sail	0850	0905	0940	1015	1115	1205	1320
2nd Sail	1515	1530	1605				

   Assuming both sails took the same time, at what time would the 2nd sail reach the Floral Gardens ?

5. a How many days are there in :- (i) June   (ii) August ?

   b How many months are there in 4 years ?

   c How many days are there in total in 2018 and 2019 ?

   d How many days (*including both dates*) are there between :-

       (i) 29th of April and 5th of May

       (ii) 16th of June and the 11th of July ?

6 Times Table

Multiplying by 6.
The 6
times table.

You should now know the :-

2 **times** table,
3 **times** table,
4 **times** table,
5 **times** table,
8 **times** table,
10 **times** table.

The 6 **times** table can be found in a similar way.

1. **Copy** and complete the green list, showing 6 sets of 5 etc.

2. Now **copy** and complete the list in the blue box, to get your 6 times table.

6 sets of 0 = 0
6 sets of 1 = 6
6 sets of 2 = 12
6 sets of 3 = 18
6 sets of 4 = 24
6 sets of 5 = ...
6 sets of 6 = ...
6 sets of .. = ...
6 sets of .. = ...
6 sets of .. = ...
6 sets of .. = ...
6 sets of 11 = ...
6 sets of 12 = ...

$0 \times 6 = 0$
$1 \times 6 = 6$
$2 \times 6 = 12$
$3 \times 6 = 18$
$4 \times 6 = 24$
$5 \times 6 = 30$
$6 \times 6 = ...$
$.. \times 6 = ...$
$.. \times 6 = ...$
$.. \times 6 = ...$
$.. \times 6 = ...$
$.. \times 6 = ...$
$.. \times 6 = ...$

Exercise 1

1. **Copy** and **complete** :-

a $3 \times 6 =$

b $5 \times 6 =$

c $2 \times 6 =$

d $4 \times 6 =$

e $6 \times 6 =$

f $7 \times 6 =$

g $10 \times 6 =$

h $8 \times 6 =$

i $9 \times 6 = $.

2. What numbers are **missing** ?

a $.... \times 6 = 12$

b $.... \times 6 = 24$

c $.... \times 6 = 36$

d $.... \times 6 = 54$

e $.... \times 6 = 0$

f $.... \times 6 = 42$

g $.... \times 6 = 48$

h $.... \times 6 = 30$

i $.... \times 6 = 60$.

3. a Martha's mum hands her a few coins.

When she looks, she has **six 2 pence** coins.

How much money does Martha have ?

b  Heather makes a **6 kilometre** round trip to the gym each day.

How far does she travel in a week (**7 days**) ?

c This steak costs **£4** in the butcher's.

Mrs Arnold bought **6** steaks.

How much did they cost her ?

d   Each glass door in my house has **9** panes.

If I have **6** glass doors, how many panes in total ?

e Marlyn works from **9** am until **5** pm, Monday to Saturday inclusive.

How many hours does she work in the week ?

4. **Copy** and **complete** :-

a 6 × 91

```
  9 1
×   6
─────
_ _ 6
```

b 47 × 6

```
  4 7
× ₄6
─────
_ 8 2
```

c
```
  14
× 6
────
```

d
```
  53
× 6
────
```

e
```
  67
× 6
────
```

f
```
  29
× 6
────
```

g
```
  43
× 6
────
```

h
```
  37
× 6
────
```

i
```
  62
× 6
────
```

j
```
  86
× 6
────
```

k
```
  97
× 6
────
```

5. Set down and work out :-

   a 71 × 6   b 58 × 6   c 6 × 49

   d 96 × 6   e 65 × 6   f 6 × 99.

6. This beaker holds **45** ml of liquid.

   How many ml in **6** beakers ?

7.  Ken has scored **27** each time he has thrown a dart for the past **6** darts.

   What is his total score for these darts ?

8. A packet of Tolos weighs **39** grams.

   What's the weight of **6** packets ?

9. An orange grower plants **70** trees in a row.

   How many trees in **6** rows ?

10. A set of car mats costs **£6**.

    A car rental company put these mats in each of its **68** cars.

    What did this cost the company ?

11.  There are **52** weeks in a year.

    How many weeks in **6** years ?

12. To work out 2 x 8 x 6 .... Do 2 x 8 = 16, then **set down** and find 16 x 6 = **96**.

    Try these :-

    a 2 x 5 x 6   b 2 x 9 x 6   c 3 x 4 x 6

    d 3 x 8 x 6   e 4 x 5 x 6   f 4 x 8 x 6

    g 5 x 5 x 6   h 10 x 8 x 6   i 6 x 6 x 6.

7 Times Table

You should now know the :-

    2 times table,
    3 times table,
    4 times table,
    5 times table,
    6 times table,
    8 times table,
    10 times table.

The 7 times table can be found in a similar way.

1.   Copy and complete the green list, showing 7 sets of 5 etc.

2.   Now copy and complete the list in the blue box, to get your 7 times table.

7 sets of 0 = 0	0 x 7 = 0
7 sets of 1 = 7	1 x 7 = 7
7 sets of 2 = 14	2 x 7 = 14
7 sets of 3 = 21	3 x 7 = 21
7 sets of 4 = 28	4 x 7 = 28
7 sets of 5 = ...	5 x 7 = 35
7 sets of 6 = ...	6 x 7 = ...
7 sets of .. = ...	7 x 7 = ...
7 sets of .. = ...	.. x 7 = ...
7 sets of .. = ...	.. x 7 = ...
7 sets of .. = ...	.. x 7 = ...
7 sets of 11 = ...	.. x 7 = ...
7 sets of 12 = ...	.. x 7 = ...

Exercise 2

1.   Copy and complete :-

    a   4 x 7 =   b   2 x 7 =   c   6 x 7 =

    d   3 x 7 =   e   5 x 7 =   f   10 x 7 =

    g   9 x 7 =   h   7 x 7 =   i   8 x 7 =   .

2.   What numbers are missing ?

    a   .... x 7 = 28   b   .... x 7 = 14   c   .... x 7 = 35

    d   .... x 7 = 21   e   .... x 7 = 49   f   .... x 7 = 56

    g   .... x 7 = 63   h   .... x 7 = 70   i   .... x 7 = 42.

3. a Thomas took a **7** at each of the first **3** holes on the putting green.

   What was his total score for these holes ?

   b  The temperature in Preston one day last spring was **6°** Celsius.

   That day in Cyprus, it was **7** times hotter.

   What was the temperature in Cyprus ?

   c Mr Flannigan hired **7** taxis to take guests to his daughter's wedding.

   If each taxi had **5** people in it, how many people in total were taken to the wedding in these taxis ?

   d  **Nine** times last year Miss Baines won **£7** at the bingo.

   How much were her total winnings ?

4. **Copy** and **complete** :–

   a 7×71

   $$\begin{array}{r} 7\,1 \\ \times\ 7 \\ \hline \_\,\_\ 7 \end{array}$$

   b 64×7

   $$\begin{array}{r} 6\,4 \\ \times\ _2 7 \\ \hline \_\ 4\,8 \end{array}$$

   c $\begin{array}{r} 28 \\ \times\ 7 \\ \hline \end{array}$

   d $\begin{array}{r} 45 \\ \times\ 7 \\ \hline \end{array}$

   e $\begin{array}{r} 76 \\ \times\ 7 \\ \hline \end{array}$

   f $\begin{array}{r} 17 \\ \times\ 7 \\ \hline \end{array}$

   g $\begin{array}{r} 34 \\ \times\ 7 \\ \hline \end{array}$

   h $\begin{array}{r} 26 \\ \times\ 7 \\ \hline \end{array}$

   i $\begin{array}{r} 69 \\ \times\ 7 \\ \hline \end{array}$

   j $\begin{array}{r} 88 \\ \times\ 7 \\ \hline \end{array}$

   k $\begin{array}{r} 94 \\ \times\ 7 \\ \hline \end{array}$

5. Set down and work out :-

    a   74 x 7   b   83 x 7   c   7 x 49

    d   95 x 7   e   67 x 7   f   7 x 99.

6. Claire has bought **15** DVD's every month
   for the past **7** months.

   How many DVD's has she bought in that time ?

7.    It costs **£7** to sign a visitor into the
                           leisure club.

                           If you take **30** visitors over the year,
                           how much will it cost ?

8. The Rovers were given **26** yellow cards last season.

   This season, they have had **7** times that !

   How many yellow cards have they had this time ?

9.    There are **59** signals between Cotton Road
                           Station and Queen's Cross.

                           Donald the train driver travels this
                           route **7** times per day.

                           How many signals does he pass in total ?

10. A car park has **7** levels.

    Each level can take **97** cars.

    How many cars altogether can the car park take ?

11. To work out 2 x 8 x 7 .... Do 2 x 8 = 16, then **set down** and find 16 x 7 = 112.

    Try these :-

    a   2 x 4 x 7   b   2 x 9 x 7   c   3 x 5 x 7

    d   3 x 9 x 7   e   4 x 6 x 7   f   4 x 10 x 7

    g   5 x 12 x 7   h   10 x 10 x 7   i   7 x 7 x 7.

Multiplying by 2, 3, 4, 5, 6, 7, 8 and 10.

Example 1 :-   354 × 6 ?

$$\begin{array}{r} 3\,5\,4 \\ \times \ _3\,_26 \\ \hline 2\,1\,2\,4 \ \checkmark \end{array}$$

Example 2 :-   429 × 7.

$$\begin{array}{r} 4\,2\,9 \\ \times \ _2\,_67 \\ \hline 3\,0\,0\,3 \ \checkmark \end{array}$$

Exercise 3

1. **Copy** and **complete** :-

a	35 × 4	b	47 × 3	c	52 × 6	d	69 × 7

e	481 × 7	f	537 × 6	g	549 × 8	h	239 × 6

i	763 × 2	j	175 × 6	k	382 × 7	l	296 × 5

2. **Set down** as in Question 1 and work out the answers :-

    a   75 × 5   b   87 × 6   c   96 × 8   d   77 × 7

    e   996 × 10   f   769 × 6   g   486 × 7   h   535 × 8.

3. Work out :-

    a   3 × 4 × 5   b   6 × 7 × 8   c   7 × 5 × 2   d   4 × 8 × 5

    e   10 × 6 × 7   f   7 × 9 × 4   g   7 × 7 × 7   h   8 × 8 × 8.

4. A tin of soup is on sale at **79** pence.

    What is the cost of **8** tins ?

5. Mr Chapman has a computing class of **28** pupils.

He bought a **£3** memory stick for each of them.

What did it cost him ?

6. A light bulb company sells **679** bulbs per hour on the internet.

One day, the internet went down for **7** hours.

How many light bulb sales did the company lose that day ?

7. Gerry the joiner has just sealed a contract in which he is to be paid **£895** per week for a period of **4** weeks.

How much will he earn altogether ?

8.  A bar of chocolate weighs **128** grams.

What is the weight of **7** bars ?

9. A syndicate of **6** factory workers won **£519** each in the Lotto.

How much was their total winnings ?

10.  **Five** adults paid **£476** each to stay in the Falcon Country Club over the weekend.

What was their total bill ?

11. The Butler family bought **3** slices of cherry pie at **86p** per slice and **4** slices of lemon tart at **50p** per slice.

How much change did they get from **£5** (500p) ?

12.  **One half** of all the people who were at the football match supported the away team.

There were **945** away supporters.

How many people in total were at the match ?

Revisit - Review - Revise

1. Copy and complete :-

    a 6 × 7 =   b 4 × 6 =   c 3 × 9 =

    d 5 × 5 =   e 7 × 7 =   f 6 × 9 = .

2. What numbers are missing ?

    a 7 × .... = 56   b 10 × .... = 370   c 6 × .... = 48

    d 4 × .... = 28   e 3 × .... = 18   f 5 × .... = 45.

3. Copy and complete these multiplications :-

    a   75   b   89   c   293
          × 6   × 7   × 4

    d   619   e   183   f   429
          × 3   × 6   × 7

4. Daisy can play 76 notes per minute on her piano.

    How many notes can she play in a 6 minute practice ?

5.   Joseph has 764 five pence coins.

    How many pence does he have altogether ?

6. George cycled 67 kilometres each day
   for a period of 4 days.

    How far did he travel ?

7. 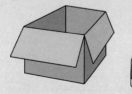 A box contains 24 cans of cola.

    6 shelves in a storeroom each have 7 boxes
    sitting on them.

    How many cans of cola are there in the room ?

Chapter 6

Integers

Be able to work with integers, negative numbers in particular.

An **integer** is simply a negative or a positive whole number including zero.

Examples :-

-2, -58, 16, 0, 149, -3871, 300 etc. are all **integers**.

5.8, $4\frac{1}{2}$, -6.2, -3.675, $-54\frac{3}{10}$ etc. are **not** integers.

The most obvious place to see positive and negative numbers is on a thermometer.

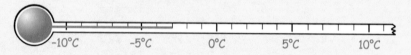

-10°C   -5°C   0°C   5°C   10°C

This thermometer shows a temperature of **-3°C**

Exercise 1

1. A thermometer is the most obvious place to see positive and negative numbers.

   What temperatures are shown here ?

   a
   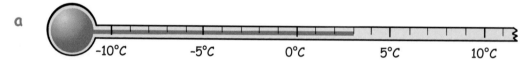
   -10°C   -5°C   0°C   5°C   10°C

   b

   -10°C   -5°C   0°C   5°C   10°C

   c
   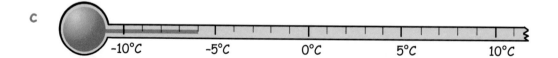
   -10°C   -5°C   0°C   5°C   10°C

   d

   -20°C   -10°C   0°C   10°C   20°C

1. e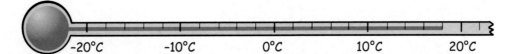

f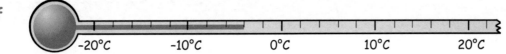

g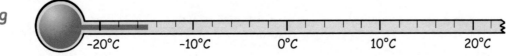

h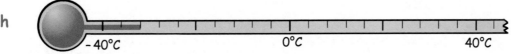

2. Write all the numbers from **0** down to **-10** in order.

3. Write down the missing numbers :-

   a   -1, -2, ..., -4, ... , -6

   b   -7, -6, ... , -4, ... , -2, -1

   c   -11, -12, ... , -14, ... , -16

   d   -20, -18, ... , -14, ... , ... ,

   e   -50, ... , -30, -20, ... , ... ,

   f   -175, -170, ... , ... , ... ,   -150.

4. Make **six** copies or tracings of the thermometer shown below.

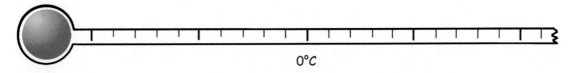

   Show each of the following temperatures on your copies :-
   (*You will need to be careful with the scale on d, e and f*)

   a   5°C

   b   -2° C

   c   -8° C

   d   -20° C

   e   -100° C

   f   -55° C.

5. Draw a large thermometer or integer number line for your classroom or for the length of the corridor outside.

Negative Numbers & the Thermometer

The thermometer down the side of the page can be a great help when studying negative numbers.

Be able to use a thermometer to help with negative numbers.

Exercise 2

1. a   Make a neat copy of this thermometer.

    b   Write down the temperature shown.

2. Look at your thermometer.

    What is the temperature that is :–

    a   2°C up from 7°C

    b   2°C up from 0°C

    c   8°C up from 3°C

    d   7°C down from 10°C

    e   12°C down from 10°C

    f   3°C up from –1°C

    g   5°C down from –3°C

    h   10°C up from –3°C

    i   7°C down from 4°C

    j   8°C down from 0°C

    k   2°C down from –7°C

    l   6°C down from –5°C

    m   8°C up from –11°C

    n   8°C up from –12°C ?

3. Can you see that 6°C is **14°C up from** –8°C.

    Copy and complete these in the same way :–

    *(State whether it's .. **up from** or .. **down from** each time)*

    a   5°C is .....°C up from 3°C

    b   2°C is .... from 7°C

    c   0°C is .... from 12°C

    d   6°C is .... from –2°C

    e   –8°C is .... from 0°C

    f   3°C is .... from –10°C

    g   –11°C is .... from –12°C

    h   –3°C is .... from 8°C

    i   10°C is ...... from –10°C

    j   –20°C is .... from –30°C.

The thermometer shows markings: 12, 11, 10, 9, 8, 7, 6, 5, 4, 3, 2, 1, 0, –1, –2, –3, –4, –5, –6, –7, –8, –9, –10, –11, –12

4.

One winter's day in Newcastle, the temperature was –8°C.

In Luton it was 2°C colder.

What was the temperature in Luton ?

5. As I left my hotel room in Birmingham the temperature was 12°C.

When I stepped outside sixty seconds later, the cold temperature of –5°C hit me immediately !

What was the difference in temperatures over those sixty seconds ?

6. Whilst on holiday, I noticed the temperature rose from –2°C at night to 12°C in late morning.

By how much had the temperature risen ?

7. At midday, the temperature in the West Midlands was –2°C.

By 4 pm, the temperature was showing as –6°C.

Had the temperature risen or fallen, and by how much ?

8. The temperature on a particular day in London was 5°C.

   a In Yorkshire the temperature was 5°C lower.

     What was the temperature in Yorkshire ?

   b In Cumbria the temperature was 9°C lower than in London.

     What was the temperature in Cumbria ?

   c It was 3°C lower in Inverness than it was in Cumbria.

     What was the temperature in Inverness ?

9. Write each set of temperatures in order, **coldest** first :-

   a 8°C, –3°C, –10°C, 0°C, 1°C, –1°C

   b –8°C, –9°C, –15°C, –20°C, 2°C, –2°C.

10. Find the **coldest** recorded temperature :-

   a in your town   **b** in the UK

   c on Earth   **d** in space.

The 3 Я's — Revisit - Review - Revise

1. State what temperatures are represented on these thermometers :-

a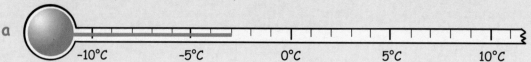

b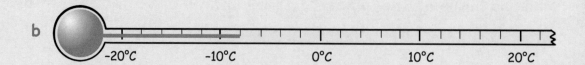

c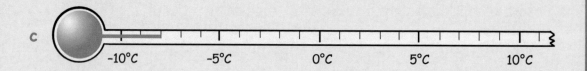

d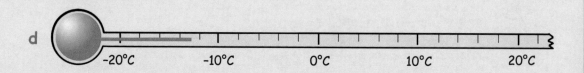

2. What is the temperature :-

   a   2°C up from 11°C

   b   5°C down from 8°C

   c   3°C up from −5°C

   d   7°C down from 4°C ?

3. The temperature at midday on a Spanish beach was 34°C.

   At midnight it had fallen to −2°C.

   By how many degrees had the temperature fallen ?

4. Write each list in order, starting with the coldest first :-

   a   7°C,   12°C,   -2°C,   0°C,   1°C,   -4°C

   b   43°C,   -16°C,   20°C,   11°C,   -11°C,   -21°C.

5. Which integer is halfway between :-

   a   7 and 11   b   -5 and - 9   c   -1 and -13 ?

 **Division 1**

Dividing by 6

Dividing by 6 sometimes with a remainder.

Remember your 6 times table ?

1 x 6 = 6	2 x 6 = 12	3 x 6 = 18	4 x 6 = 24
5 x 6 = 30	6 x 6 = 36	7 x 6 = 42	8 x 6 = 48
9 x 6 = 54	10 x 6 = 60	11 x 6 = 66	12 x 6 = 72

Example 1 :-

72 ÷ 6

72 ÷ 6 = **12**

from knowing the 6 times table.

Example 2 :-

107 ÷ 6

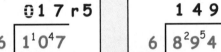

$$\begin{array}{r} 0\,1\,7\;r\,5 \\ 6\overline{)1^{1}0^{4}7} \end{array}$$

Example 3 :-

894 ÷ 6

$$\begin{array}{r} 1\,4\,9 \\ 6\overline{)8^{2}9^{5}4} \end{array}$$

Example 4 :-

913 ÷ 6

$$\begin{array}{r} 1\,5\,2\;r\,1 \\ 6\overline{)9^{3}1^{1}3} \end{array}$$

Exercise 1

1. **Copy** and **complete** :-

    a   54 ÷ 6 = ...   b   48 ÷ 6 = ...   c   34 ÷ 6 = ...

    d   27 ÷ 6 = ...   e   43 ÷ 6 = ...   f   52 ÷ 6 = ...

    g   66 ÷ 6 = ...   h   57 ÷ 6 = ...   i   28 ÷ 6 = ...

2. **Set down** and **work out** :-

    a 6)62   b 6)18   c 6)68   d 6)76

    e 6)80   f 6)60   g 6)47   h 6)79

    i 6)91   j 6)96   k 6)42   l 6)99 .

3. **Copy** and **complete** :-

    a 6⟌100   b 6⟌105   c 6⟌204   d 6⟌214

    e 6⟌108   f 6⟌302   g 6⟌222   h 6⟌447

    i 6⟌408   j 6⟌528   k 6⟌508   l 6⟌810 .

4. **Set these down** like Question 3 and find the answers :-

    a $96 \div 6 = ...$ b $38 \div 6 = ...$ c $94 \div 6 = ...$

    d $606 \div 6 = ...$ e $570 \div 6 = ...$ f $725 \div 6 = ...$

5. Try these questions **mentally**.

    a I have just eaten **6** packets of sweets.

        54 sweets altogether.

        How many sweets were in a packet ?

    b   Young Eck has **42** bricks.

        How many towers of **6** can he make ?

    c Mrs Young takes **36** books out of a box and divides them into sets of **6**.

        How many sets ? 

Set down these questions as division sums and work them out.

6. An elephant is allowed **6** bags of hay each day.

    How many days would it take the elephant to munch through **72** bags ? 

7. There are **75** fish to be put in equal numbers into **6** tanks.

    How many fish go in each tank and how many will need to go in an extra tank ? 

8. Emma shared out **84** strawberry chunks
    among **herself** and **five** pals.

    How many did they each get ?

9.   **90** tins of paint are laid out on **6** shelves.

    How many tins are on each shelf ?

10. You can get **6** people into a canoe.

    How many canoes will be needed for **100** people ?

11. Sally paid **£288** to hire a car for **6** days.

    How much was that per day ?

12. A cash and carry warehouse packs **260** packets of soap
    powder into **6** boxes.

    How many go in each box and how many are left over ?

13.  **6** men go to a football match and pay **£210**
    in total to get in.

    How much did it cost for each of them ?

14. There are **510** pieces of cutlery in a restaurant.

    At a function, everyone needs **6** pieces of cutlery.

    How many people are attending the function ?

15.  A watering can holds **6** litres of water.

    I used **460** litres of water to water my plants.

    How many times did I completely fill the watering
    can and how many litres of water were in the can
    for the final watering ?

16. I have **6** boxes, each with **6** packets of marbles.

    If in total, there are **864** marbles, how many must there be in each packet ?

Dividing by 7

Dividing by 7 sometimes with a remainder.

Remember your 7 times table ?

1 x 7 = 7	2 x 7 = 14	3 x 7 = 21	4 x 7 = 28
5 x 7 = 35	6 x 7 = 42	7 x 7 = 49	8 x 7 = 56
9 x 7 = 63	10 x 7 = 70	11 x 7 = 77	12 x 7 = 84

Example 1 :-

35 ÷ 7

35 ÷ 7 = 5

from knowing the 7 times table.

Example 2 :-

93 ÷ 7

$$\begin{array}{r} 1\ 3\ r\ 2 \\ 7\ \overline{)\ 9\ ^2 3} \end{array}$$

Example 3 :-

868 ÷ 7

$$\begin{array}{r} 1\ 2\ 4 \\ 7\ \overline{)\ 8\ ^1 6\ ^2 8} \end{array}$$

Example 4 :-

964 ÷ 7

$$\begin{array}{r} 1\ 3\ 7\ r\ 5 \\ 7\ \overline{)\ 9\ ^2 6\ ^5 4} \end{array}$$

Exercise 2

1. Copy and complete :-

    a   21 ÷ 7 = ...

    b   28 ÷ 7 = ...

    c   17 ÷ 7 = ...

    d   38 ÷ 7 = ...

    e   56 ÷ 7 = ...

    f   50 ÷ 7 = ...

    g   63 ÷ 7 = ...

    h   61 ÷ 7 = ...

    i   84 ÷ 7 = ...

2. Set down and work out :-

    a   7)73   b   7)14   c   7)69   d   7)42

    e   7)53   f   7)35   g   7)79   h   7)82

    i   7)90   j   7)70   k   7)96   l   7)88

    m   7)99   n   7)91   o   7)77   p   7)98 .

3. **Copy** and **complete** :-

   a $7\overline{)103}$ b $7\overline{)106}$ c $7\overline{)126}$ d $7\overline{)383}$

   e $7\overline{)266}$ f $7\overline{)459}$ g $7\overline{)343}$ h $7\overline{)619}$

   i $7\overline{)604}$ j $7\overline{)539}$ k $7\overline{)903}$ l $7\overline{)917}$.

4. **Set these down** like Question 3 and find the answers :-

   a $112 \div 7 = $ ....   b $439 \div 7 = $ ....   c $413 \div 7 = $ ....

   d $510 \div 7 = $ ....   e $649 \div 7 = $ ....   f $896 \div 7 = $ ....

5. Try these questions **mentally**.

   a   My skirt was **7** times dearer than my top.

   My skirt cost **£56**.

   What did I pay for my top ?

   b    Joe has **42** bananas which he shares between **himself** and **six** friends.

   How many do they each get ?

   c   Scarves are on sale at **£7** each.

   How many can be bought for **£63** ?

Set down these questions as division sums and work them out.

6. A caterer has **91** packets of tea which she empties into **7** containers.

   How many containers does she fill ?

7. Buses are lined up in the garage in rows of **7**.

   How many rows will there be when there are **89** buses in the garage and how many will be in a row of their own ?

8. Gherkins are put into jars, **7** in each jar.

If there are **128** gherkins, how many jars will be needed and how many extra gherkins will there be ?

9. **177** seniors turn up to play **seven**-a-side rugby.

How many teams can be formed ?

10.  There are **322** seats on **7** coaches.

How many seats on each coach ?

11. Blank CD's come in packs of **7**.

If I had **185** CD's how many packs did I have and how many loose ones were there ?

12.  A cruise ship has **7** levels with **903** passengers spread out evenly throughout each level.

How many people are on each level ?

13. Rose bushes cost **£7** each.

A gardener had **£576** to spend on rose bushes.

How many could he buy and how much had he left over ?

14.  Sugar mice are priced **7** pence each in a shop.

The shop takes in £8 and 68 pence (**868** pence) from the sale of sugar mice.

How many must it have sold ?

15. Penguins are allowed **7** fish per feed.

A zoo has a stock of **587** fish.

How many feeds will this last and how many fish left over ?

16. I checked and found there are **651** calories in **7** candy bars.

How many calories are there in each bar ?

Exercise 3

Be able to divide up to a 3 digit number by 2, 3, 4, 5, 6, 7, 8 or 10.

1. **Copy** and **complete** :-

   a $\overset{3\ ....}{2\overline{)7^18}}$ b $3\overline{)54}$ c $4\overline{)68}$ d $5\overline{)75}$

   e $6\overline{)66}$ f $7\overline{)98}$ g $8\overline{)96}$ h $10\overline{)90}$

   i $5\overline{)620}$ j $6\overline{)258}$ k $3\overline{)636}$ l $2\overline{)512}$

   m $7\overline{)329}$ n $4\overline{)168}$ o $10\overline{)740}$ p $8\overline{)280}$

   q $6\overline{)672}$ r $3\overline{)744}$ s $7\overline{)476}$ t $8\overline{)408}$.

There are several ways of asking, for example, ... how to **divide 91 by 7**.

Here are some of them :-

| 91 divided by 7 | $7\overline{)91}$ | 7 into 91 | 91 ÷ 7 | $\dfrac{91}{7}$ |

---

2. Write the following in the form $3\overline{)78}$ and then work out the answer :-

   a   78 ÷ 3   b $7\overline{)133}$ c $\dfrac{96}{6}$

   d   104 divided by 8   e   4 into 516   f   225 ÷ 5

   g $\dfrac{288}{8}$ h $2\overline{)778}$ i   6 into 768

   j   608 divided by 4   k $\dfrac{252}{7}$ l   904 ÷ 8.

3. **Show all of your working** in each of these problems :-

a   There are **85** people waiting at a taxi rank.

     If a taxi can hold **5** people, how many taxis are needed ?

b   Coco the clown gave away **90** balloons to children.

     Each child received **6** balloons

     How many children must there have been ?

c   Mrs Moyer paid **£528** for **3** identical single beds for her children.

     What was the price of each bed ?

d   Grandpa gave out **72** sweets to be shared amongst his **4** grandchildren.

     How many sweets did they get each ?

e   A crisp company has **238** packets of crisps to be put into jumbo packs with **7** packets in each.

     How many jumbo packs can be made up ?

f   I read **342** pages of my book over **6** days, reading the same number of pages each day.

     How many pages did I read each day ?

g   A toy store took in **£232** selling **8** identical games consoles.

     What is the price of each console ?

h   A prize of **£427** was split amongst **10** young ladies.

     How many £'s did each get and how much had to be changed into pennies ?

i   Molly Bun baked **732** pancakes for a jamboree.

     She gave **half** to the scouts and **half** to the cubs.

     How many pancakes did the cubs get ?

The 3 Я's

1. Copy and complete :-

   a 6) 54   b 7) 49   c 6) 73   d 7) 45

   e 2) 156   f 3) 267   g 4) 516   h 5) 375

   i 6) 720   j 7) 903   k 8) 904   l 8) 921.

2. Write in the form 7) 84   and work out the answer :-

   a 84 ÷ 7   b 6 into 42   c 103 divided by 6

   d $\dfrac{544}{8}$ e 708 ÷ 4   f 3 into 771.

3. It cost £138 for Jake and his 5 friends to get into an amusement park.

   What was the cost for one ?

4. The train fare for a group of 7 adults came to £525.

   What was the cost per person ?

5.  192 oranges are to be packed in nets, 8 to each net.

   How many nets will be needed ?

6. Joyce put 130 grams of sugar, 6 eggs and 100 grams of flour into a mixture.

   If the total weight of the mixture was 572 grams and the six eggs weighed the same, what was the weight of one egg ?

 Chapter 8

9 Times Table

Multiplying by 9.
The 9
times table.

You should now know the :-

   2 times table,
   3 times table,
   4 times table,
   5 times table,
   6 times table,
   7 times table,
   8 times table
   10 times table.

The **9** times table can be found in a similar way.

a   **Copy** and complete the green list, showing 9 sets of 5 etc.

b   Now **copy** and complete the list in the blue box, to get your 9 times table.

9 sets of 0 = 0	0 x 9 = 0
9 sets of 1 = 9	1 x 9 = 9
9 sets of 2 = 18	2 x 9 = 18
9 sets of 3 = 27	3 x 9 = 27
9 sets of 4 = 36	4 x 9 = 36
9 sets of 5 = ...	5 x 9 = 45
9 sets of 6 = ...	6 x 9 = ...
9 sets of .. = ...	7 x 9 = ...
9 sets of .. = ...	.. x 9 = ...
9 sets of .. = ...	.. x 9 = ...
9 sets of .. = ...	.. x 9 = ...
9 sets of 11 = ...	.. x 9 = ...
9 sets of 12 = ...	.. x 9 = ...

Exercise 1

1.   **Copy** and **complete** :-

   a   9 x 3 =   b   9 x 2 =   c   9 x 6 =

   d   9 x 4 =   e   9 x 7 =   f   9 x 5 =

   g   9 x 8 =   h   9 x 10 =   i   9 x 9 =

2.   What numbers are **missing** ?

   a   9 x .... = 0   b   9 x .... = 45   c   9 x .... = 9

   d   9 x .... = 63   e   9 x .... = 81   f   9 x .... = 27

   g   9 x .... = 90   h   9 x .... = 72   i   9 x .... = 54.

3. a This handbag was in a sale, priced **£5**.

   Henry bought **9** of them for his nieces.

   How much did he spend ?

b  Toilet rolls come in packs of **6**.

   Marjory bought **9** packs.

   How many toilet rolls did she buy ?

c Beryl can get **8** good sized slices from this fruit loaf.

   She has baked **9** loaves.

   How many good sized slices will she get altogether ?

d Janet drinks **9** cups of coffee every day.

   How many cups of coffee will she have had over **7** days ?

e A new fizzy drink can be bought in packs of **9**.

   Jak stocks up by buying **9** packs.

   How many cans has Jak bought ?

4. **Copy** and **complete** :-

a   9 x 61

```
    6 1
  x   9
 ----------
 .... .... 9
```

b   73 x 9

```
    7 3
  x ₂9
 --------
 .... 5 7
```

c   15
    x 9
   ____

d   24
    x 9
   ____

e   36
    x 9
   ____

f   47
    x 9
   ____

g   51
    x 9
   ____

h   76
    x 9
   ____

i   84
    x 9
   ____

j   88
    x 9
   ____

k   97
    x 9
   ____

5. Set down and work out :-

   a   19 x 9   b   21 x 9   c   56 x 9

   d   9 x 82   e   9 x 77   f   9 x 63.

6. Noreen used her washing machine **9** times per week over **28** weeks last winter.

   How many times was that altogether ?

7.  Rexall Stores took on **9** new employees in each of its **46** stores.

   How many people in total did the company take on ?

8. Old Jock plays golf on **72** days of the year.

   He only plays **9** holes each time.

   How many holes does he play in the year ?

9.  A lawyer produces a **nine** page document which she sends to **69** fellow lawyers.

   How many pages did she have to run off ?

10. Mary Baker always puts **9** large bits of chocolate chip into her chocolate chip muffins.

    How many bits does she use for **50** muffins ?

11. A shop has **63** boxes of luxury chocolates on display.

    They cost **£9** per box.

    How much is this display worth ?

12. Over his time as a judge he reckons that he has given a **9** month sentence to **99** criminals.

    How many months is that in total ?

Multiplying a 3
digit number
by 8 or 9.

Example 1 :-   276 × 8.

```
  2 7 6
× 6 4 8
───────
2 2 0 8  ✓
```

Example 2 :-   359 × 9.

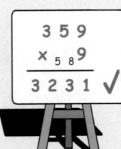

```
  3 5 9
× 5 8 9
───────
3 2 3 1  ✓
```

Exercise 2

1. **Copy** and **complete** :-

a   213
      × 8
   ─────

b   174
      × 9
   ─────

c   385
      × 6
   ─────

d   462
      × 7
   ─────

e   519
      × 9
   ─────

f   678
      × 9
   ─────

2. **Set down** as in Question 1 and work out the answers :-

a   107 × 9

b   265 × 8

c   389 × 7

d   613 × 6

e   884 × 9

f   963 × 9.

3. A recipe states that **146** grams of butter
    is needed to make a cake.

    If a baker is to make **8** cakes, how many
    grams of butter does she need ?

4.

A restaurant held an eat-all-you-can-eat
buffet for **£9** per person.

How much money did the restaurant take in
on a day when **239** customers came in ?

Mixed Exercise

Exercise 3

1. **Copy** and **complete** each calculation :-

   a 62
      × 6

   b 93
      × 7

   c 81
      × 8

   d 57
      × 9

   e 276
      × 2

   f 145
      × 3

   g 897
      × 4

   h 319
      × 5

2. A hotel serves **3** rashers of bacon on each breakfast plate.

   67 people turn up for breakfast.

   How many rashers of bacon are needed ?

   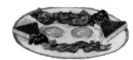

3.

   A ticket for the circus costs **£5**.

   If **94** tickets are sold one evening, how much money did the circus make ?

4. A school bought in **68** packets of pencils.

   Each packet had **6** pencils in it.

   How many pencils did the school buy in total ?

5.

   These tennis balls come in packs of **4**.

   A tennis club bought **17** packs.

   How many balls in total is that ?

6. Sandy usually pays **£49** per month for his car insurance, but the insurance company gave him **2** months free.

   How much of a saving was that ?

7. a Find the answer to 2 x 3 x 4 x 5 x 6.

   b Find the answer to 6 x 7 x 8 x 9 x 10.

8. Each pot of flowers contains **9** marigolds.

How many marigolds has a garden centre with **45** pots ?

9.  A baker's shop has only **7** cup cakes left for sale.

Mary buys them all at **98p** each.

What did it cost her ?

10. A piece of cake has **389** calories in it.

How many calories are there in **6** pieces of this cake ?

11.  There are **4** shelves of cereal in a supermarket.

Each shelf has **237** packets on it.

How many packets of cereal in total ?

12. A jet can travel **569** miles in an hour.

How many miles can it travel in **5** hours ?

13. There are **382** dimples on a golf ball.

How many dimples will there be on **6** golf balls ?

14. A supermarket has **259** boxes of candles on sale.

Each box has **8** candles in it.

How many candles altogether does the supermarket have ?

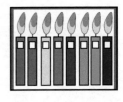

15.  **225** ml of fresh orange is needed to make up 1 litre of a cocktail.

How much would be needed to make **10** litres of the cocktail ?

1. Copy and complete :-

   a   9 x 6 =   b   8 x 7 =   c   9 x 10 =

   d   8 x 9 =   e   12 x 9 =   f   4 x 9 x 3 = .

2. What numbers are missing ?

   a   5 x .... = 45   b   10 x .... = 4200   c   8 x .... = 64

   d   7 x .... = 63   e   6 x .... = 480   f   9 x .... = 630.

3. Copy and complete these multiplications :-

   a   87   b   209   c   165
          x 9   x 6   x 7
         ─────   ─────   ─────

   d   269   e   748   f   163
          x 8   x 3   x 9
         ─────   ─────   ─────

4. A garden centre has 157 wheelbarrows of plants,
   for sale, with 8 plants growing in each barrow.

   How many plants altogether are being used ?

5.  A zoo has 86 tanks of tropical fish.

   There are 9 fish in each tank.

   How many tropical fish does the zoo have in total ?

6. These boxes of chocolates contain 24 chocolate macaroons.

   There are 7 shelves of them on display
   in a chain of 9 supermarkets.

   How many single macaroons are on display ?

Chapter 9

Reading Coordinate Grids

Coordinates 1

Be able to identify the position of an object on a coordinate grid.

The position of an object can be described by using a

COORDINATE GRID.

The position can be given by showing which **square** the object is sitting in.

The position of the **dog** is **Bd**.

The **cat** is at **Eb**.   The **mouse** is at **Cc**.

Always go **along** first, then **up**.

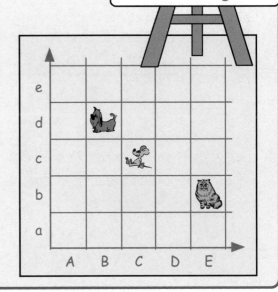

Exercise 1

1.   Look at the grid shown.

Write the position of :-

a   the **elephant**   b   the **panda**

c   the **tiger**   d   the **giraffe**

e   the **monkey**   f   the **lion**.

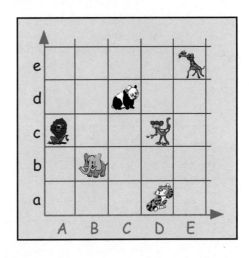

2.

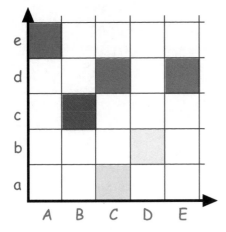

Look at the grid shown.

Write the position of the :-

a   blue square   b   **green** square

c   red square   d   **brown** square

e   pink square   f   grey square

g   white squares in row d.

3.

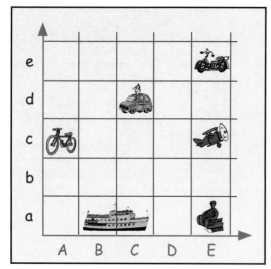

a   What is at position **Cd** ?

b   What is at **Ac** ?

c   What is at **Ec** ?

d   What is at **Ba** and **Ca** ?

e   What is at **Ea** ?

f   What is at **Ee** ?

4. This grid shows plots in a large field where the farmer keeps his crops and his animals.

a   Write the position of **each plot**. (*example* : ducks - B1)

b   Write the positions of each pink square of the **pathway**.

c   Write the positions of the **empty plots**.

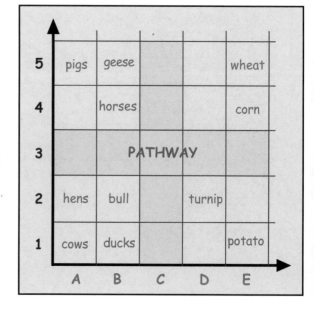

5.

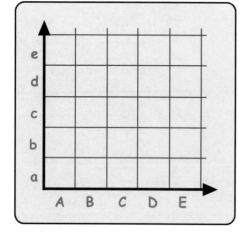

Copy the grid shown.

a   Colour these squares **blue** :-
    Bd, **De**, **Ea** and **Ae**.

b   Colour these squares **red** :-
    Ce, **Cc**, **Aa** and **Ec**.

6. Copy the grid from question 5.

a   This time, make a pattern of your own, using colours.

b   For each square you coloured in, write down its colour and its grid position.   (***Example*** : red - B2).

7. Shown is a group of islands where Pirates are said to hide treasure.

*Notice the **Harbour** on **Rock Island** is at **D8**.*

a Write down the position of the Harbour on :-

   (i) Marsh Island

   (ii) Volcano Island

   (iii) Palm tree Island

   (iv) Waterfall Island.

b Write down the position of the :-

   (i) lighthouse

   (ii) dock

   (iii) waterfalls

   (iv) icebergs

   (v) palm trees.

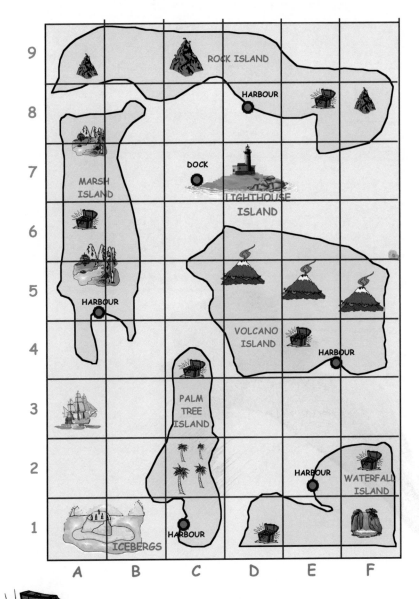

c Write down the position of all six treasure chests.

d What island is on :-

   (i) C9   **(ii)** F5   **(iii)** A6   **(iv)** A3 ?

e A pirate ship sails from the harbour on Waterfall Island to the Harbour on Rock Island.

   Describe the ship's journey using the grid references it might pass through.

Reading Coordinates on Grid Lines

Be able to identify the position of an object on coordinate grid lines.

The position of an object or point can also be described by using

COORDINATE GRID LINES.

This shows the **2 lines** where the point lies.

Examples :-

- The position of the dog **C5**.
- The position of the cat is **F3**.

Remember :- along first, then up.

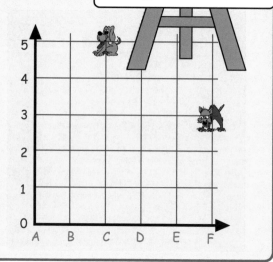

Exercise 2

1. Six subject rooms in a school are shown on the coordinate grid.

   Write down the position of :-

   a   Mathematics **M**   b   English **E**

   c   Geography **G**   d   History **H**

   e   Art **A**   f   Computing **C**.

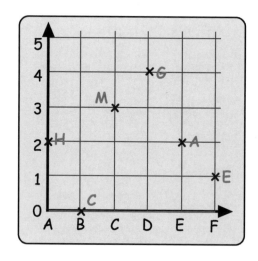

2.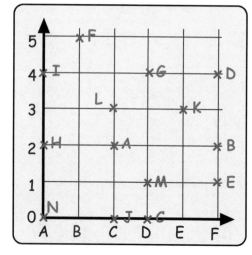

   a   Write down the grid coordinates of each letter in this grid.
   (e.g. A is at C2).

   b   From point A, what letter is :-

   (i)   one right and 2 up

   (ii) 3 right and one down ?

   c   Name the letters lying on grid line :-

   (i) **D**   (ii) **2**.

3.

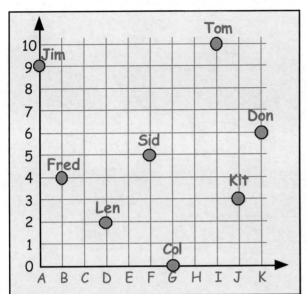

Eight soldiers are out on a training exercise in a field.

Name the soldier who is in position :-

a   D 2   b   B 4

c   A 9   d   J 3

e   K 6   f   F 5

g   I 10   h   G 0.

4. At the school fayre, Joyce was in charge of a stall where you could win cash prizes.

You had to push a pin through a hole on a piece of card.

Some of the holes had no prizes !

Example :-

· if you push a pin through **B1**, you **win £1**,

· if you push a pin through **C0**, you **lose**.

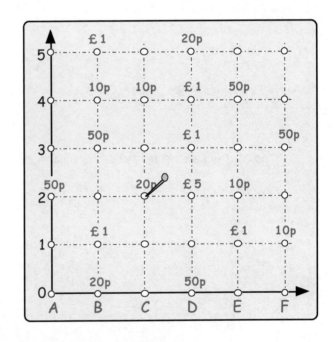

a   What did you win if you pushed the pin through position :-

(i) **D3**   (ii) **E4**   (iii) **B2**   (iv) **F3**   (v) **D5**   (vi) **A0** ?

b   Which positions gave a **10p** prize ? (List all of them).

c   What was the top prize and what was its position ?

5. Why do you think that using coordinate **grid lines** is better than using coordinate **boxes** ?

1. A 10p coin rolling board has the prizes as shown.

   If you roll a coin and it lands inside D2 you win **50p**.

   a   What would you win if your 10p coin landed on :-

   (i)   **B1**   (ii)   **E3**

   (iii)   **A5**   (iv)   **E4** ?

   b   List 5 other grid references where you would **NOT** win a prize.

   c   Where would you win :-   (i)   **20p**   (ii)   **1p**   (iii)   **£2** ?

2. Fantasy Island is shown on the grid.

   a   Write down what is at :-

   (i)   **Bc**   (ii)   **Be**

   (iii)   **Dd**   (iv)   **Ea**.

   b   Write down the grid reference for the :-

   (i)   Caves   (ii)   Port

   (iii)   Harbour   (iv)   Swamp.

   The roads on the island follow the grid lines.
   From the Port to the City you would go through **Ce, Cd, Cc** then **Bc**.

   c   Describe which references you might go through to go from the Harbour to the Caves by land.

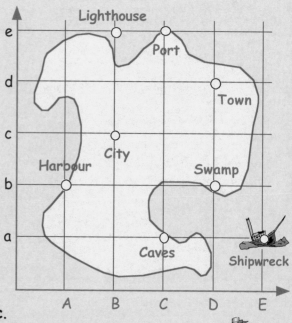

Chapter 10

Division 2

Dividing by 9

Dividing by 9 sometimes with a remainder.

Remember your 9 times table ?

1 x 9 = 9	2 x 9 = 18	3 x 9 = 27	4 x 9 = 36
5 x 9 = 45	6 x 9 = 54	7 x 9 = 63	8 x 9 = 72
9 x 9 = 81	10 x 9 = 90	11 x 9 = 99	12 x 9 = 108

Example 1 :-

72 ÷ 9

72 ÷ 9 = 8

from knowing the 9 times table.

Example 2 :-

118 ÷ 9

$$0\ 1\ 3\ r1$$
$$9\ \overline{)\ 1\ ^1 1\ ^2 8}$$

Example 3 :-

954 ÷ 9

$$1\ 0\ 6$$
$$9\ \overline{)\ 9\ 5\ ^5 4}$$

Example 4 :-

976 ÷ 9

$$1\ 0\ 8\ r4$$
$$9\ \overline{)\ 9\ 7\ ^7 6}$$

Exercise 1

1. **Copy** each of these and **complete** :-

   a   27 ÷ 9 = ...   b   18 ÷ 9 = ...   c   9 ÷ 9 = ...

   d   54 ÷ 9 = ...   e   45 ÷ 9 = ...   f   63 ÷ 9 = ...

   g   81 ÷ 9 = ...   h   72 ÷ 9 = ...   i   90 ÷ 9 = ...

   j   36 ÷ 9 = ...   k   99 ÷ 9 = ...   l   108 ÷ 9 = ...

2. **Set down** and **work out** :-

   a   9$\overline{)36}$ b   9$\overline{)24}$ c   9$\overline{)61}$ d   9$\overline{)54}$

   e   9$\overline{)76}$ f   9$\overline{)72}$ g   9$\overline{)68}$ h   9$\overline{)71}$

   i   9$\overline{)105}$ j   9$\overline{)93}$ k   9$\overline{)96}$ l   9$\overline{)87}$.

3. Copy and **complete** :-

a 9)103   b 9)171   c 9)116   d 9)234

e 9)406   f 9)414   g 9)527   h 9)585

i 9)780   j 9)792   k 9)873   l 9)918 .

4. **Set these down** like Question 3 and find the answers :-

a 67 ÷ 9 = ...   b 126 ÷ 9 = ...   c 79 ÷ 9 = ...

d 314 ÷ 9 = ...   e 672 ÷ 9 = ...   f 783 ÷ 9 = ...

5. Try these questions **mentally**.

a Auntie Ida spent **£45** on her nieces at Christmas.

   She gave each of them a **£9** voucher for HVM Stores.

   How many nieces does she have ?

b   Ian spent a total of **£54** buying **9** magazines.

   How much were they each ?

c These jars can hold **9** large cookies and keep them fresh.

   Donna has made **63** large cookies.

   How many jars will she need ?

Set down these questions as division sums and work them out.

6. One evening, Jenny played skittles and managed
   to get **9** points every time she bowled.

   If she scored **108** points altogether,
   how many times did she roll a bowl ?

7.   A football club orders **100** second hand footballs online.

   If it has **9** teams, from under 10's to seniors, how many
   balls will each team get if they get the same amount and
   how many balls will not be used yet ?

8. Alistair paid the **£621** he owed on his car in equal payments over a period of **9** months.

    What did he pay each month ?

9.  Each newspaper contains **9** pages of sport.

    If a company runs off **945** pages of sport, how many newspapers will it have run off ?

10. Recipe books are on sale at **£9** each.

    If a catering school has **£292** left to spend, how many of these books can it order and how much money will the school be left with ?

11.  A company director paid **£324** in total for **9** of his customers to have a day's golf.

    How much did he pay for each of them ?

12. **Nine** fishermen agreed to share their catch.

    Altogether they caught **240** fish.

    How many did they each get and how many could be given to the gulls ?

13.  Timothy moves **525** books from the store to a classroom.

    If he could only manage **9** books at a time, how many trips did he have to make and how many books did he carry on his last trip ?

14. Airport luggage handlers load **756** pieces of luggage onto an aircraft.

    They divide them equally into **9** crates.

    How many pieces of luggage are in each crate ?

15.   Cement is on special offer at **£9** for **packs of three**.

    How many single packs will I get for **£162** ?

Mixed Problems using +. –, × and ÷

Exercise 2

1. **Copy, set down** and **work out** :-

   a   42 + 27

   b   89 – 64

   c   2 × 12

   d   56 ÷ 8

   e   103 – 78

   f   76 + 89

   g   108 ÷ 9

   h   8 × 12

   i   205 + 172

   j   864 – 451

   k   98 ÷ 7

   l   6 × 16

   m   5 into 450

   n   278 + 417

   o   600 – 24

   p   9 × 78

   q   368 – 209

   r $8\overline{)608}$

   s   1345 + 2456

   t   7819 – 3741

   u   4 × 357

   v $\dfrac{744}{3}$

   w   8400 + 1600

   x   10 000 ÷ 10.

In the following questions, you have to decide whether each problem involves **adding**, **subtracting**, **multiplying** or **dividing**.

Show all of your working

When you have decided, carry on and solve the problem.

---

2. **305** buses were due to bring supporters to the cup final.

   Major roadworks meant that only **118** of them arrived in time for the kick -off.

   How many buses didn't make it on time ?

3. Three ships left Portsmouth just after 7 am, bound for France.

   The St Malo ferry left with **158** passengers on board.

   The Cherbourg ferry had **276** and the ferry to Le Havre carried **87**.

   How many passengers **altogether** were on these three ships ?

4. George the mechanic serviced **605** cars this year compared to **489** last year.

   How many more cars did he service this year ?

5. Mrs Fluff dusts every room in the house **every day** of the week.

   How many times is that over a period of **28** weeks ?

6. A group of **9** people agreed to share their winnings when they went on a work's day out to Cheltenham Races.

   How much did they each get if they won a total of **£783** ?

7. **200** women were asked if they preferred to rent a mobile phone or use "pay as you go".

   96 said rent, **85** said "pay as you go" and the rest said they did not have a mobile phone.

   How many women did not have one ?

8. Simon has **three 50** pence coins, **five 10** pence coins and **twenty** **2** pence coins.

   How much does he have altogether in pence ?

9.  A dog breeder had **50** mother bulldogs.

   Over a period, **38** of them had **6** puppies each, while the rest each had **3** puppies.

   How many puppies were born at that time ?

10. **Eight** ladies each have **7** daughters and each of these daughters have **4** children.

    How many grandchildren altogether do the ladies have ?

11.  **875** bananas were to be shared among **5** gorillas over a **week**.

    Each gorilla had to be fed the same amount each day.

    How many bananas was that each day ?

1. Copy and **complete** :-

   a 9⟌27   b 9⟌72   c 9⟌108   d 9⟌104

   e 8⟌632   f 7⟌696   g 6⟌654   h 5⟌387

   i 4⟌868   j 3⟌972   k 9⟌807   l 8⟌790 .

2. Write in the form 9⟌81   and work out the answer :-

   a 81 ÷ 9   b 9 into 63   c 110 divided by 9

   d $\dfrac{684}{9}$ e 696 ÷ 8   f 6 into 744.

3. Jamie bought 9 identical CD's for £153.

   How much were they each ?

4.    A banana costs 23p and a pineapple costs 89p.

   How many pennies for 4 bananas and 5 pineapples ?

5. Anne spent £365 on her dress. Mary spent £175 on hers.

   a   What did the two of them spend altogether ?

   b   How much more than Mary did Anne spend ?

6. 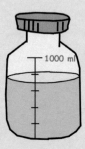 Jessie poured out 75 ml of weed killer from a bottle
   which contained 700 ml.

   The weed killer which was left in the bottle was
   then poured equally into 5 watering cans.

   How much was in each can ?

What is a Decimal Number ?

Be able to read, interpret and write a decimal number.

Earlier, we considered whole numbers made up of Units (or 1's), Tens, Hundreds and Thousands.

When you take a single unit and split it into 10 (or 100 or 1000) bits, what we then have are called **decimal fractions** of a whole number.

For example, take a rectangular bar of chocolate as our "UNIT" of measure.

If we divide it into 10 equal "bits",

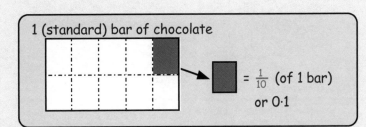

1 (standard) bar of chocolate

= $\frac{1}{10}$ (of 1 bar)

or 0·1

each bit is $\frac{1}{10}$ of the bar and is written as 0·1. ← 1 "tenth"

In the decimal number 5·7, the "7" refers to 7 **tenths** or $\frac{7}{10}$.

Unit tenth
U   t
5 · 7

Exercise 1

1. In this question, stands for 1 (whole number).

    What do the following diagrams represent ?

    a   b   c

    d 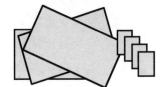   e 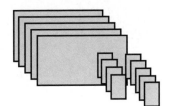   f

2. Draw neat pictures, in the same style as shown above, to represent :–

    a 0·4   b 1·8   c 2·3   d 6·2.

3. Shown here is part of a circle.

   It has been divided into 10 sections.

   What decimal number does the pink part represent ?

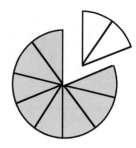

4. What decimal numbers are represented in the following diagrams ?

   a

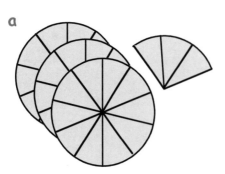

   b

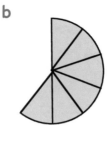

   c

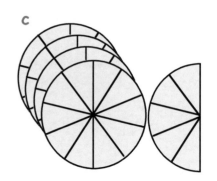

The Second Decimal Place

When our 1 bar of chocolate was divided into 10 pieces, each bit was called 1 tenth ($\frac{1}{10}$).

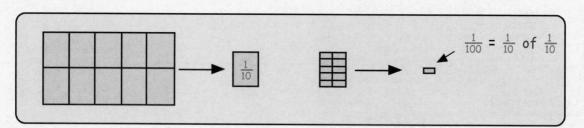

=> when a "tenth" is then cut into 10 equal bits each bit is ($\frac{1}{10}$ of $\frac{1}{10}$) = $\frac{1}{100}$.

   In the decimal number,

   5·76, the "6" refers to 6 **hundredths** or $\frac{6}{100}$.

Unit	tenth	hundredth
U	t	h
5 ·	7	6

---

5. What numbers are represented in the diagrams below ?

   a

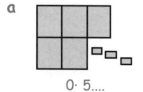

   0· 5....

   b

   0· ......

   c

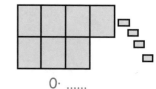

   0· ......

5. d 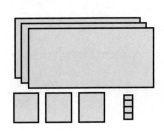 e 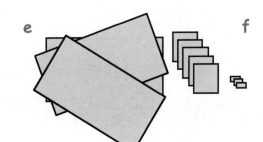 f

6. Draw neat pictures to show the following decimal numbers :-

    a 0·35   b 1·72   c 3·81   d 0·05.

7. In the decimal number 26·89, what does the :-

    a **8** represent   b **2** represent   c **9** represent   d **6** represent ?

8. What does the **7** represent in each of these numbers :-

    a 72·18   b 235·72   c 57·02   d 26·37 ?

9. What does the **9** represent in these numbers :-

    a 91·42   b 19·26   c 45·98   d 61·39 ?

10. Arrange the following numbers in order, **smallest** first :-

    a 0·85,   1·06,   0·07,   0·94,   0·04,   1·21

    b 0·12   0·21   0·1   0·2   0·09   0·22.

11. What number is :-

    a 0·1 up from 1·6   b $\frac{1}{10}$ down from 5·7   c $\frac{3}{10}$ up from 4·2

    d $\frac{7}{10}$ up from 0·15   e 0·03 up from 1·17   f $\frac{1}{100}$ down from 2·85

    g $\frac{2}{100}$ down from 1·87 h $\frac{5}{100}$ up from 2·44   i $\frac{10}{100}$ down from 1·15 ?

12. What number lies **half way** between :-

    a 0·3 and 0·5   b 0·8 and 1·0   c 2·2 and 2·8

    d 4·3 and 4·7   e 5·4 and 5·5   f 0·1 and 0·2 ?

One Decimal Place

Before deciding which number an arrow is pointing to, first look at the 2 whole numbers which lie on either side of the arrow.

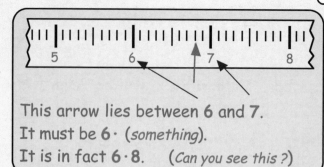

This arrow lies between **6** and **7**.

It must be **6·** (*something*).

It is in fact **6·8**.   (*Can you see this ?*)

Exercise 2

1.   Write down the number each of these arrows is pointing to :–

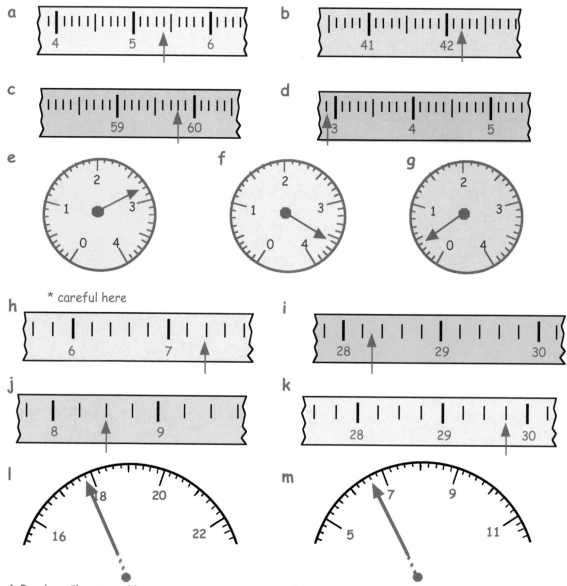

a

4   5   6

b

41   42

c

59   60

d

3   4   5

e

2
1   3
0   4

f

2
1   3
0   4

g

2
1   3
0   4

h   * careful here

6   7

i

28   29   30

j

8   9

k

28   29   30

l

18   20
16   22

m

7   9
5   11

2 Decimal Places (Harder)

Firstly, look at the 2 numbers shown on the scale which lie either side of the arrow, the **6·5** and **6·6**.

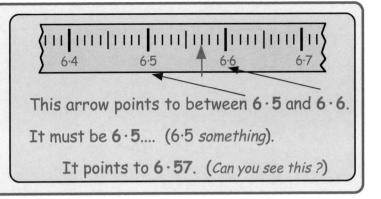

This arrow points to between **6·5** and **6·6**.

It must be **6·5....** (*6·5 something*).

It points to **6·57**. (*Can you see this ?*)

2.   To which numbers are each of the following arrows pointing ?

a
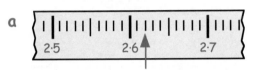

b

c
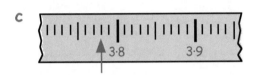

d
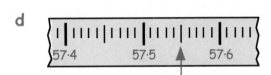

e
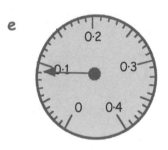

f
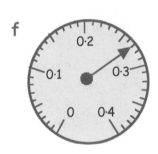

g
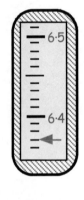

h   * careful here
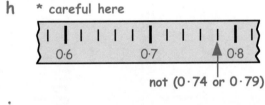

not (0·74 or 0·79)

i

j

k

l

m

3. To which numbers are the arrows pointing?

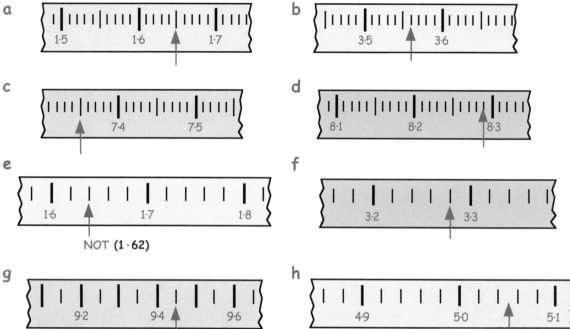

a

b

c

d

e

NOT (1·62)

f

g

h

i

j

k

l

m

n

o

p

4. Look at the scale below and write down what numbers the arrows A, B, C..... are pointing to.

1. What decimal numbers are represented by these diagrams ?

   a   b

   (this represents 1 whole unit)

2. Draw diagrams (similar to question 1) to represent :-

   a 1·3   b 0·7   c 2·64   d 3·02.

3. In the decimal number 63·85, what does the :-

   a 6 represent   b 5 represent   c 8 represent   d 3 represent ?

4. Write down the number that is :-

   a 0·2 up from 5·6   b 0·04 down from 3·76

   c $\frac{7}{10}$ down from 5·8   d $\frac{2}{10}$ up from 8·0.

   e $\frac{5}{100}$ down from 3·27   f $\frac{9}{100}$ up from 0·76.

5. What number is halfway between :-

   a 0·5 and 0·9   b 1·2 and 1·8   c 0·64 and 0·68 ?

6. Arrange each list in order, smallest first :-

   a 1·7,   1·09,   1·47,   2,   1·18,   1·01

   b 4·75,   4·8,   5·62,   5·08,   4·9,   5·2.

7. What decimal numbers are the arrows pointing to ?

   a   b

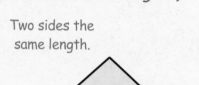

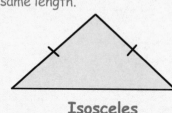

Define a triangle depending on the lengths of its sides.

Side Properties :-   There are **3 types of triangles** (*based on their side lengths*).

All 3 sides different lengths.

Two sides the same length.

All 3 sides the same length.

Scalene   **Isosceles**   **Equilateral**

Exercise 1

1. a   Trace or make a neat copy of this triangle.

   b   **Copy** and **complete** :-

   "A triangle which has all 3 sides different in length is called a .... triangle".

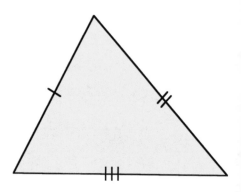

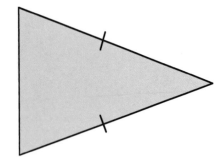

2.   a   Trace or make a neat copy of this triangle.

   b   **Copy** and **complete** :-

   "A triangle which has 2 of its sides equal in length is called an .... triangle".

3. a   Trace or make a neat copy of this triangle.

   b   **Copy** and **complete** :-

   "A triangle which has all 3 sides the same length is called an .... triangle".

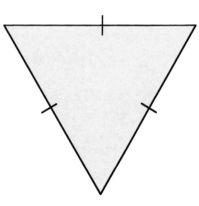

Year 4 Book - Chapter 12   page 92   Geometry 1

4. State which **type** of triangle each of the following is :-

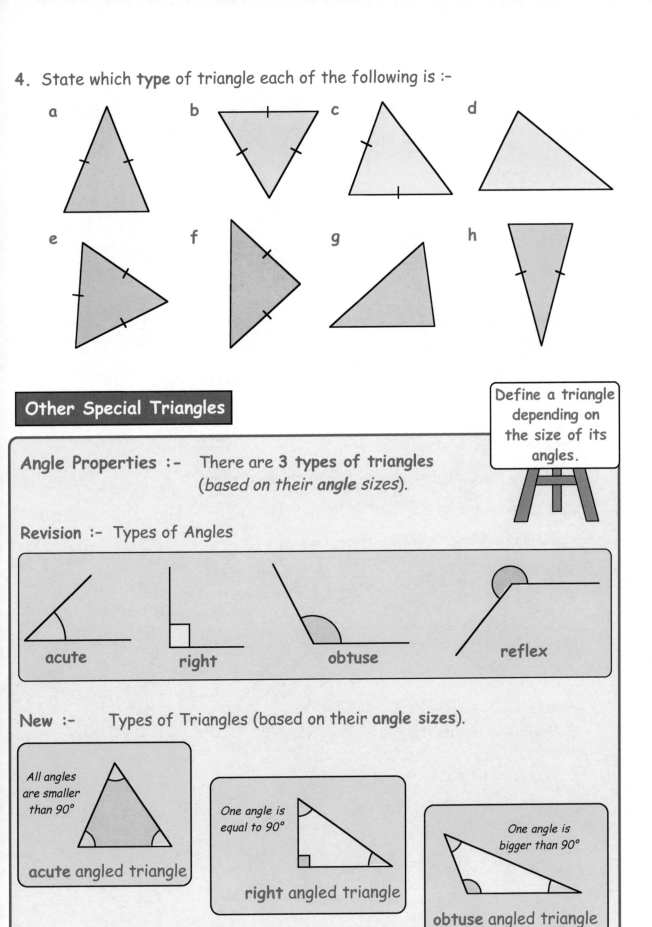

a   b   c   d

e   f   g   h

Other Special Triangles

Define a triangle depending on the size of its angles.

Angle Properties :- There are **3 types of triangles** (*based on their angle sizes*).

Revision :- Types of Angles

acute   right   obtuse   reflex

New :- Types of Triangles (based on their **angle sizes**).

All angles are smaller than 90°

acute angled triangle

One angle is equal to 90°

right angled triangle

One angle is bigger than 90°

obtuse angled triangle

1. State whether each of the following is an **acute** angled, **right** angled or **obtuse** angled triangle :-

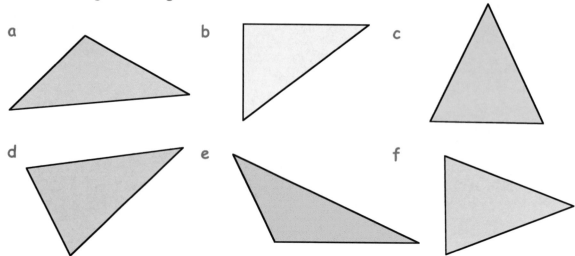

a   b   c

d   e   f

2. Naming triangles using **3 letters**.

The **vertices** (corners) of this triangle are **A**, **B** and **C**.

It is called **triangle ABC** (or △ABC for short.)

Name each of the following triangles.

Use **CAPITAL** letters :-

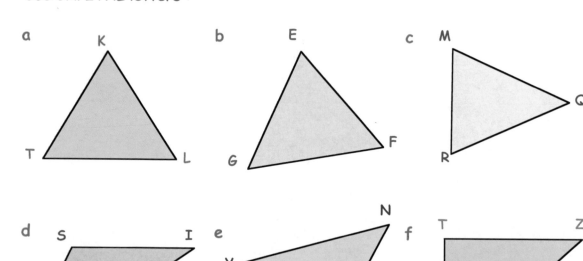

a   b   c

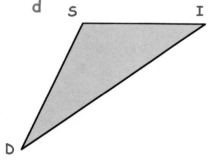
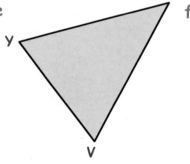
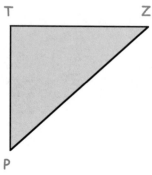

d   e   f

Describing a Triangle Fully

Describing a triangle, based on both its sides and its angles.

A triangle can now be **fully** described as follows :-

Step 1 ⟶ **Step 2** ⟶ **Step 3**

Name it using :-
3 letters

Describe it as :-

  (i)   acute-angled
  (ii) right-angled
  (iii) obtuse-angled

Followed by :-

  (i)   isosceles triangle
  (ii) equilateral triangle
  (iii) scalene triangle

Example :-   Triangle DEF is an **obtuse angled isosceles** triangle.

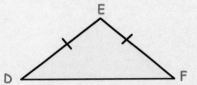

Exercise 3

1. Describe this triangle in the same way :-

   "Δ............ is a .... angled .... triangle".

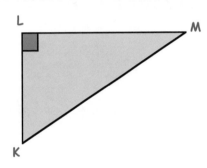

2.

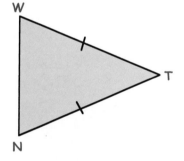

Describe this triangle in the same way :-

   "Δ............ is an .... angled .... triangle".

3. Describe each of the following triangles in the same way :-

a 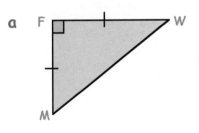   b 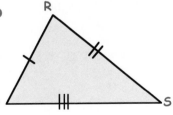   c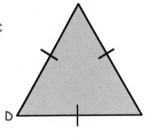

d 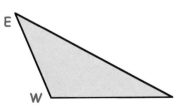   e 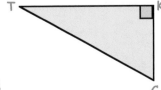   f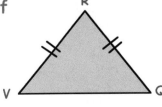

1. Describe each of these triangles by using an expression from this list.

a

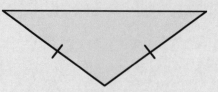

scalene triangle
isosceles triangle
equilateral triangle

b 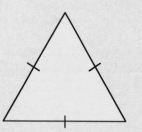   c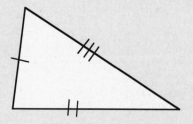

2. Describe each of these triangles by using an expression from this new list.

a

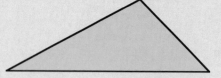

right angled
acute angled
obtuse angled

b 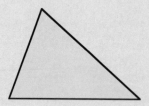   c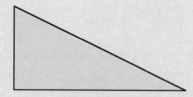

3. Name both of these triangles and then describe them fully.

a 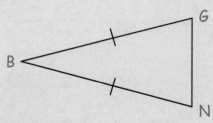   b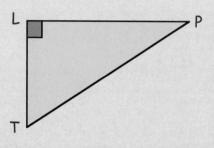

Be able to find the position of a point using a grid system.

The Coordinates of a Point

The position of an object or point can be described by using a (*Cartesian*) **Coordinate Grid System**.

The position of a point is given by stating which **two lines** the point is on.

Remember the following :-

- always start at point **O**, go **ALONG** first, then **UP**.
- always put **BRACKETS** round the two numbers.
- always put a **COMMA** between the two numbers.

Example :-

To find the coordinates of point **M** :-

-> Start at **O**,

go 3 boxes **ALONG**,

then go 4 boxes **UP**.

"**M** is the point **(3,4)**", or

"the coordinates are given as **M(3,4)**".

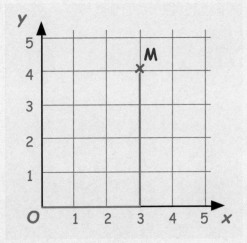

Notes :- the point O(0, 0) is called the **ORIGIN**.

the "**ALONG**" arrowed line is called the *x*-axis.

the "**UP**" arrowed line is called the *y*-axis.

1. Five locations in an airport
   shopping centre are shown
   in the coordinate grid.

   Write down the coordinates of :-

   a   the fashion store **F**

   b   the travel agents **T**

   c   the bike shop **B**

   d   the games shop **G**

   e   the pizza place **P**

   f   the Odeon Cinema **O**.

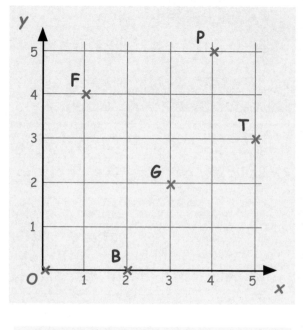

2. Write down the capital letter
   representing each point and
   put its coordinates next to it.

   Example :-   G(2, 6).

3.

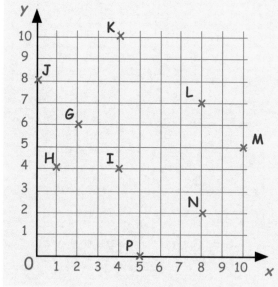

a   Which point has coordinates :-

   (i)   (6, 10)   (ii)   (0, 3)

   (iii) (3, 2)   (iv)   (9, 4) ?

b   Write down the coordinates of :-

   (i)   F   (ii)   D

   (iii) K   (iv)   L

   (v)   N   (vi)   C.

3. c Four of the points can be joined to form a square.

     (i) Which four points ?   **(ii)** Write down their coordinates.

4. Now it's your turn to plot points.

   a Draw a coordinate grid like the one in question 3 on squared paper. Make the horizontal and vertical axes both go from 0 to 10.

   b Mark with a small neat cross the position of the following points :-

     A(0, 3),   B(3, 2),   C(5, 0),   D(8, 3),   E(7, 4),   F(10, 6),

     G(8, 7),   H(5, 9),   I(1, 10),   J(2, 7),   K(9, 1),   L(1, 5).

   c Join point J to point H; join point H to point G; join point G to point C. Now join point C to point J.

   d What shape have you formed ?

5. a Draw a new grid (from 0 to 6 in each axis).

   b Mark with a cross the following points :-

       E(2, 1) F(4, 1) G(5, 3) H(3, 5) I(1, 3).

   c When the five points are joined in order, what shape is formed ?

6. a Draw a new grid (from 0 to 6 in each axis).

   b Mark with a cross the following points :-

       J(3, 4) K(0, 1) L(5, 1) M(0, 4) N(3, 0) J(3, 4) .

   c When the points are joined in order, what shape is formed ?

7. Make up your own diagrams and coordinates that form shapes. Test your friends.

More about the x-axis and y-axis

Use mathematical language to give the position of a point.

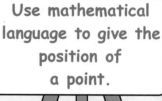

Remember :-

• the grid used is a **Cartesian coordinate grid.**

• the point **O**(0, 0) is called the **origin.**
  This is where the *x*-axis meets the *y*-axis.

• the **horizontal** axis (*the "along" axis*)
  is called **the *x*-axis.**

• the **vertical** axis (*the "up" axis*)
  is called **the *y*-axis.**

RULE :- | Start at **O**, go ALONG the *x*-axis first, then go UP.

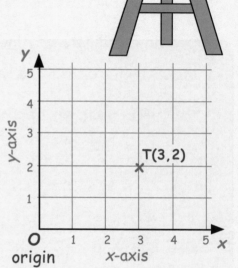

Exercise 2

1. Look at the coordinate grid shown opposite.

   Each time you mention a point, write what fruit is at that point.

   a   Which point has an *x*-coordinate of 5 ?

   b   Which point has a *y*-coordinate of 2 ?

   c   What is the :-

   (i) *x*-coordinate of **U**   (ii) *y*-coordinate of **S** ?

   d   Which points have their *x*-coordinate the same as their *y*-coordinate ?

   e   Which point lies on the :-   (i) *x*-axis   (ii) *y*-axis ?

   f   Write down the coordinates of the 2 points which have the same :-

   (i) *y*-coordinate   (ii) *x*-coordinate.

2. Look at this coordinate grid.

a   What are the coordinates of **B** ?

b   Which point has
      coordinates (9, 8) ?

c   Which point has the same
      y-coordinate as **G** ?

d   Which point has the same
      x-coordinate as **L** ?

e   3 points have the same
      y-coordinate.

      Name them and write
      down their coordinates.

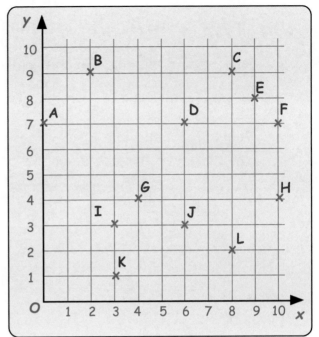

f   Which point lies on the *y*-axis ?

g   Which points have the same *x* and *y*-coordinate ?

h   Is the *y*-axis known as the horizontal axis or the vertical axis ?

3. Draw a 5 by 5 coordinate grid as shown.

a   Plot the points **P**(1, 2), **Q**(5, 2)
      and **R**(5, 4).

b   **S** is a point to be put on the grid
      so that figure **PQRS** is a **rectangle**.

      On your diagram plot the point **S**
      and write down its coordinates.

c   Join **P** to **R** and join **Q** to **S**.

      You now have the two **diagonals**
      of the rectangle.

      Write down the coordinates of the
      point where the two diagonals meet.

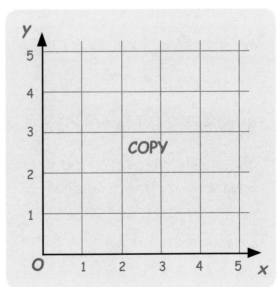

4. Draw another 5 by 5 coordinate grid as shown in question 3.

   a   Plot the points **K**(3, 1), **L**(5, 3) and **M**(3, 5).

   b   **N** is a point to be put on the grid so that figure **KLMN** is a **square**.

   On your diagram plot the point **N** and write down its coordinates.

   c   Join **K** to **M** and join **L** to **N**.
   You now have the two diagonals of the square.

   Write down the coordinates of the point where the two
   diagonals meet.

5. You will need to draw 5 more coordinate grids.
   (*Make each of them 5 by 5*).

   On separate grids :-

   •   plot each set of points.

   •   join each of them up in order.

   •   write below each one, the name of the shape you have formed.

   a   Join **A**(3, 1) to **B**(4, 1) to **C**(4, 5) to **D**(3, 5), back to **A**.

   b   Join **E**(1, 2) to **F**(3, 2) to **G**(3, 4) to **H**(1, 4), back to **E**.

   c   Join **I**(1, 4) to **J**(3, 3) to **K**(5, 4) to **L**(3, 5), back to **I**.

   d   Join **M**(0, 2) to **N**(2, 5) to **P**(4, 2) to **Q**(2, 1), back to **M**.

   e   Join **R**(5, 3) to **S**(4, 5) to **T**(2, 5) to **U**(1, 3) to **V**(3, 1) back to **R**.

   You should have found a diamond, a pentagon, a rectangle, a kite and a
   square - but not in that order !

6. Coordinates can be fun. Go to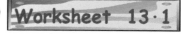

1. a   Which point has coordinates :-

        (i)   (9, 6)   (ii)   (6, 0)

        (iii) (4, 7)   (iv)   (7, 10) ?

    b   Write the coordinates of :-

        (i)   E   (ii)   G

        (iii) R   (iv)   P.

    c   When 4 of the points are
        joined a rectangle is formed.

        (i) Which 4 points ?

        (ii) Write their coordinates.

    d   Which point lies on the :-   (i) x-axis   (ii) y-axis ?

    e   Name any 2 points with :-

        (i) the same x-coordinate (ii) the same y-coordinate.

    f   Which 2 points have their x and y coordinates the same ?

2. Copy the 10 by 10 coordinate grid shown below.

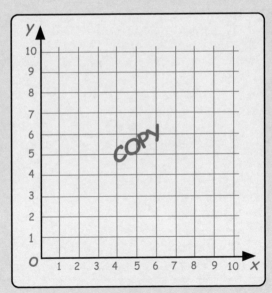

    a   Plot the points P(1, 3), Q(8, 3)
        and R(9, 7).

    b   S is a point to be put on the grid so
        that figure PQRS is a parallelogram.
        On your diagram plot the point S
        and write down its coordinates.

    c   Join P to R and join Q to S.

        Put a cross where these two diagonals
        meet and write down the coordinates
        of this point.

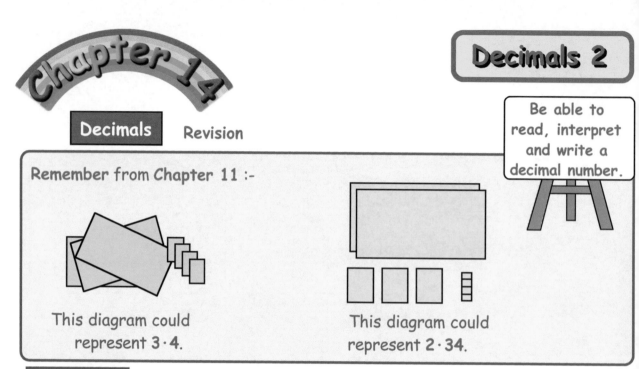

Chapter 14

Decimals 2

Decimals   Revision

Be able to read, interpret and write a decimal number.

Remember from Chapter 11 :-

This diagram could represent 3·4.

This diagram could represent 2·34.

Exercise 1

1. Write the decimal number represented by each of these diagrams :-

a

b

c

d

e

f

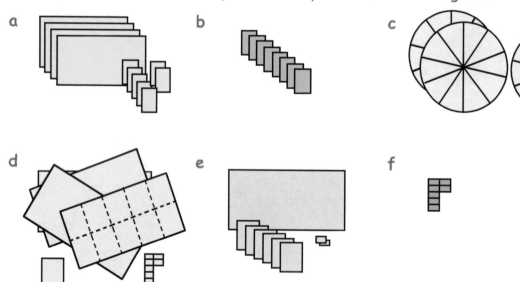

2. In the decimal number 63·857, what does the :-

   a   6 represent   b   5 represent   c   8 represent   d   7 represent ?

3. What decimal numbers are the arrows pointing to ?

a

b

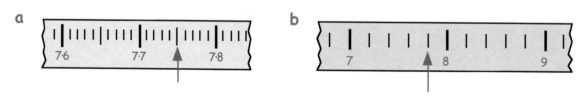

Rounding to the Nearest Whole Number

6·3

lies between **6** and **7**.

It is closer to **6**.

(*the nearest whole number*).

```
    6      6·5      7
         6·3
```

40·71

lies between **40** and **41**.

It is closer to **41**.

(*the nearest whole number*).

```
   40      40·5      41
               40·71
```

When rounding to **the nearest whole number** :-

=> look at **the first digit which comes just after the decimal point** :-

if it is a 5, 6, 7, 8 or 9 => round **up** to the next whole number.

if it is a 0, 1, 2, 3 or 4 => **leave** the whole number before the point as it is.

Examples :-   5·4 = **5** to the nearest whole number.

2·8 = **3** to the nearest whole number.

6·5 = **7** to the nearest whole number.

8·399999 = **8** to the nearest whole number.

1. When each decimal is rounded to the nearest whole
    number, which of the two numbers in the brackets
    is the correct answer :-

a   6·2   (6 or 7)   b   4·7   (4 or 5)

c   5·9   (5 or 6)   d   3·4   (3 or 4)

e   13·16   (13 or 14)   f   17·86   (17 or 18)

g   4·5   (4 or 5)   h   6·05   (6 or 7)

i   80·65   (80 or 81)   j   200·28 (200 or 201)

k   163·86 (163 or 164)   l   54·91   (54 or 55)

m   1013·49 (1013 or 1014)   n   0·62   (0 or 1) ?

2. Copy and complete these statements :-

   a   1·8 lies between 1 and 2 .   It is closer to ...

   b   3·4 lies between 3 and ...   It is closer to ...

   c   8·5 lies between ... and ...   It is closer to ...   (remember the rule)

   d   2·59 lies between ... and ...   It is closer to ...

   e   6·23 lies between ... and ...   It is closer to ...

   f   0·74 lies between ... and ...   It is closer to ...

   g   15·8 lies between ... and ...   It is closer to ...

   h   33·54 lies between ... and ... It is closer to ...

   i   69·82 lies between ... and ... It is closer to ...

3. Round these to the nearest **whole £** :-

   a   £6·20   b   £8·90   c   £4·30   d   £5·60

   e   £14·80   f   £16·50   g   £19·49   h   £17·71

   i   £0·43   j   £0·53   k   £0·50   l   £106·48.

4. Round these measurements to the nearest **whole centimetre** :-

   a   8·4 cm   b   9·6 cm   c   10·8 cm   d   3·1 cm

   e   4·47 cm   f   7·85 cm   g   18·29 cm   h   24·63 cm

   i   26·27 cm   j   38·99 cm   k   43·14 cm   l   69·50 cm.

5. Round these numbers to the nearest whole number, in the same way :-

   a   1·467 —>   b   4·972 —>   c   8·268 —>

   d   6·3486 —>   e   5·4457 —>   f   7·0593 —>

   g   14·75554 —>   h   17·07984 —>   i   29·64765 —>

Adding or Subtracting Decimals

When you add or subtract decimal numbers, it is important to

..... line up the decimal points.

Example :–   To add 3·7 and 4·62   =>

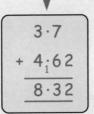

```
   3·7
+ 4ᵢ62
 ─────
  8·32
```

Exercise 3

1. Try to do the following **mentally**. Write down the answers to :-

    a   4·8 + 5·1   b   6·6 + 2·3   c   3·9 + 8·4

    d   8·7 + 3·5   e   0·34 + 0·46   f   0·49 + 0·37

    g   0·42 + 0·78   h   0·44 + 0·97   i   5·2 + 5·56

    j   4·8 – 4·5   k   9·6 – 6·2   l   8·7 – 0·6

    m   2·5 – 0·5   n   7·7 – 4·9   o   8·4 – 1·8

    p   11 – 0·86   q   3 – 0·43   r   6 + 3·7 – 2·6.

2. What is the total length of each of the following garden implements ?

    a

    18·3 cm   22·5 cm

    b

    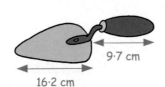

    9·7 cm

    16·2 cm

    c

    7·5 cm

    10·8 cm

3. Try the following **mentally** :-

    a   An empty cooking pot lid weighs 0·6 kilograms.

        The pot without the lid weighs 3·7 kilograms.

        (i)   What is the combined weight ?

        (ii) What is the difference in weight ?

    b   May travels 5·8 km by motorbike from her home to meet Nan.

        Nan travels 6·7 km from her home to meet May.

        After their meeting, they both return to their own homes.

        What is the **combined** distance of both their journeys ?

3. c It is 6·9 miles along the motorway from
my house to the supermarket.

If I go the scenic route, it is 9·5 miles
to the supermarket.

How much shorter is it to travel on the motorway ?

d

Three boys get pocket money from
their gran every Friday.

Bob gets £7·30, as he is the oldest.
Fred gets £5·50 and young Dave gets £3·80.

How much money does gran pay
out each week ?

4. Copy the following and find :-

a   5·6
    + 1·5

b   18·3
    + 7·9

c   13·7
    + 56·8

d   76·8
    + 24·9

e   7·65
    + 1·73

f   4·28
    + 3·09

g   13·57
    + 15·78

h   29·14
    + 3·87

i   36·94
    + 28·09

j   8·5
    - 2·3

k   43·8
    - 22·4

l   62·4
    - 35·7

m   32·48
    - 26·5

n   7·48
    - 6·35

o   8·49
    - 6·57

p   9·67
    - 4·91

q   5·02
    - 4·43

r   12·23
    - 5·34

5. **a** Letitia bought a bracelet for £45·50 and earrings at £12·65.

How much did she spend **altogether** ?

b Ralph bought a camera for £82·35
but sold it the following year for £23·70.

How much did he lose by selling the camera ?

c  In an ice skating competition, Marion was
awarded 1·9 points **more than** Christopher.

Christopher received 7·4 points.

What was Marion's mark ?

6. A delivery man is to deliver two parcels.

One weighs 19·7 kg, the other weighs 36·7 kg.

What is the **total** weight of the parcels ?

7. A lawnmower priced at £89·85 in the Garden Centre
appears on the Internet for £59·89.

How much would you save by buying online ?

8.

Adult	£8·50
Child	£5·20
Student	£6·45
Senior	£3·99

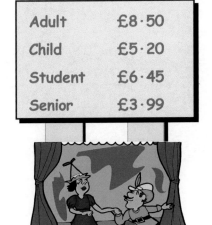

Theatre prices for an amateur society's
production of Robbie Hood are shown.

a What price for :-

(i) 1 adult and 1 child

(ii) 2 students with their mother

(iii) 4 seniors ?

b What change will you get from £20 if
you pay for six year old Joe, his
mother and his old granny ?

c Mr Dobbie paid for himself and his children, costing a total of £39·70.

How many children did he have with him ?

Revisit - Review - Revise

1. What decimal numbers are the arrows pointing to ?

   a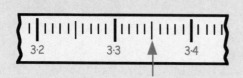

   b

2. Round the following to the nearest whole number :-

   a 6·3   b 9·8   c 71·29   d 84·817.

3. Do the following mentally (no working) :-

   a 3·8 + 6·2   b 8·3 + 4·75   c 9·5 – 3·4   d 0·92 – 0·38.

4. Copy the following and find :-

   a   4·92   b   26·65   c   9·7   d   19·76
       + 1·39   + 4·57   – 3·2   – 7·98

   e £2·96 + £5·85   f £35·39 + £4·12   g £3·75 – £3·67

   h 56·32 – 8·64   i 20 – 8·52   j 96·81 – 49·36.

5. Mavis buys a tennis skirt for £26·99 and a sweat band for £2·58.

   How much change should she receive from £30 ?

   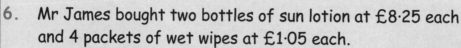

6. Mr James bought two bottles of sun lotion at £8·25 each
   and 4 packets of wet wipes at £1·05 each.

   a How much did it cost him in total ?
      (Show all your working).

   b He handed over a £20 and a £5 note.

      How much change did he get ?

Chapter 15

Geometry 2

Quadrilaterals

Be able to recognise
a quadrilateral and
know some of its
properties.

What is meant by a "Quadrilateral" ?

A "Quadrilateral" is a closed 4 sided linear shape.

The shape is made up of 4 straight lines.

You have already met most of them.

In this chapter, we examine their properties
and mention another quadrilateral, the trapezium.

Exercise 1

1. Trace or sketch each of these **quadrilaterals**, and write the name of each
   one below your sketch :-

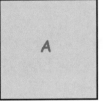 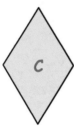  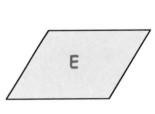

2. What do each of the 5 figures above all have in common ?

3. Let us study shape A :-

   a Again, state the name of this shape.

   b Copy and complete - "All 4 sides are the same ....".

   c Copy and complete - "The opposite sides are p...........".

   d Copy and complete - "All 4 angles are r....... a.........".

   e Copy and complete - "The shape has .... lines of symmetry".

   f If you cut the shape out of a piece of paper and are allowed to turn
      it over and rotate it, in how many ways can it fit back into the hole ?

4. Let us now study shape **B** :-

   a   Again, state the name of this shape.

   b   Copy and complete - "The opposite sides are the same ....".

   c   Copy and complete - "The opposite sides are p..........".

   d   Copy and complete - "All 4 angles are r....... a........".

   e   Copy and complete - "The shape has .... lines of symmetry".

   f   If you cut the shape out of a piece of paper and are allowed to turn
       it over and rotate it, in how many ways can it fit back into the hole ?

5. Let us look now at shape **C** :-

   a   Again, state the name of this shape.

   b   Copy and complete - "All 4 sides are the same ....".

   c   Copy and complete - "The opposite sides are p..........".

   d   Copy and complete - "The angles marked * are the .... size".

   e   Copy and complete - "The angles marked # are the .... size".

   f   Copy and complete - "The shape has .... lines of symmetry".

   g   If you cut the shape out of a piece of paper and are allowed to turn
       it over and rotate it, in how many ways can it fit back into the hole ?

6. Let us turn our attention to shape **D** :-

   a   Again, state the name of this shape.

   b   Copy and complete - "The sides marked * are the same ....".

   c   Copy and complete - "The sides marked ▢ are the same ....".

   d   Copy and complete - "The opposite sides are n..... p..........".

   e   Copy and complete - "The angles marked ◯ are the .... size".

   f   Copy and complete - "The angles marked ✫ are n..... the .... size".

   g   Copy and complete - "The shape has .... line of symmetry".

   h   If you cut the shape out of a piece of paper and are allowed to turn
       it over and rotate it, in how many ways can it fit back into the hole ?

7. Let us look now at the 5th shape **E** :-

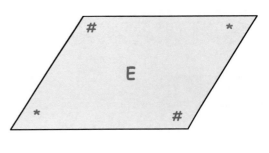

   a State the name of this shape.

      Copy and complete -

   b "The opposite sides are the same ....".

   c "The opposite sides are p..........".

   d "The angles marked * are the .... size".

   e "The angles marked # are the .... size".

   f Copy and complete - "The shape has .... lines of symmetry".

   g If you cut the shape out of a piece of paper and are allowed to turn
      it over and rotate it, in how many ways can it fit back into the hole ?

8. Here is a new **quadrilateral** :-

   a Try to find the name of this new shape.

      Copy and complete -

   b "None of the sides are the same ....".

   c "The top and bottom sides are p..........".

   d "None of the angles are the .... size".

   e Copy and complete - "The shape has .... lines of symmetry".

   f If you cut the shape out of a piece of paper and are allowed to turn
      it over and rotate it, in how many ways can it fit back into the hole ?

9. How many squares, rectangles, rhombi, kites, parallelograms and trapezia,
   (*plural of trapezium*), can you see in this picture ?

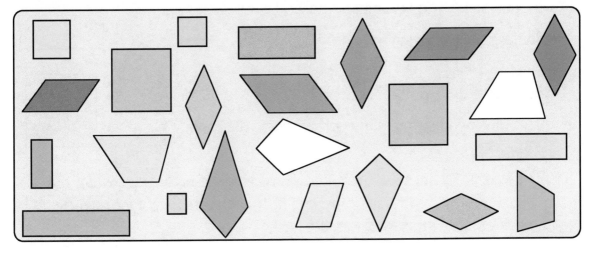

Comparing Quadrilaterals

1. In this question, some facts are given about a **quadrilateral**.

    You have to say what kind each is (*There may be more than 1 answer each time*).

    a   I have all 4 sides the same length, but only 2 lines of symmetry.

    b   My opposite sides are parallel, but I have no right angles.

    c   I have all 4 sides of different lengths.

    d   I have only 1 line of symmetry.

    e   All my angles are right angles but not all my sides are the same length.

    f   I have exactly 2 lines of symmetry.

    g   When cut out, I can fit back into the hole in 8 different ways.

    h   Only 1 pair of my opposite sides are parallel.

2. Think of all 6 **quadrilaterals** and answer these questions.

    a   Write down 2 ways in which a **square** is different from a **rectangle**.

    b   Write down 2 ways in which a **rectangle** is different from a **parallelogram**.

    c   Write down 2 ways in which a **rhombus** is different from a **kite**.

    d   Write down 2 ways in which a **square** is different from a **rhombus**.

    e   Write down 2 ways in which a **rhombus** is different from a **parallelogram**.

3. I was told to draw a **square** and here is what I drew :- ⟶

    Explain why my drawing was **wrong**.

4. I was told to draw a **rectangle** and here is what I drew :- ⟶

    Explain why my drawing is in fact **correct** this time.

5. Design a shape (a house, a boat, etc.) that is made up of several of the
    quadrilaterals you have been studying in this chapter, colour them,
    and display the best of them on the wall.

Be able to recognise regular and irregular polygons.

A "POLYGON" is a two dimensional shape with straight lines.

A polygon is "REGULAR" only if all sides are equal and all angles are equal, otherwise it is "IRREGULAR".

Examples :-   This **pentagon** is a **regular** polygon.

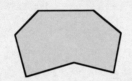

This is an **irregular** polygon.

A **polygon** (*poly* - many) usually refers to shapes with **more** than **4** sides.

1. Shown below are some **regular polygons**. The one marked C is a **pentagon**.

   Try to find the names of the others.

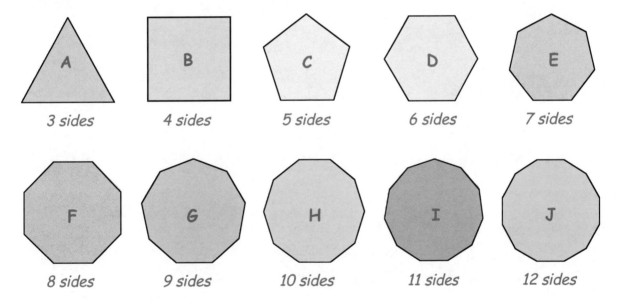

A	B	C	D	E
3 sides	4 sides	5 sides	6 sides	7 sides

F	G	H	I	J
8 sides	9 sides	10 sides	11 sides	12 sides

2. It is easy to think of lots of shapes in real life that are triangles or squares.

   a   Think of 3 things in real life that are in the shape of a **pentagon**.

   b   Which 2 **polygons** appear (or soon will appear) in our everyday coins ?

   c   Which polygon has exactly **8** lines of symmetry ?

3. Which of these **polygons** are **regular**? Write yes or no.

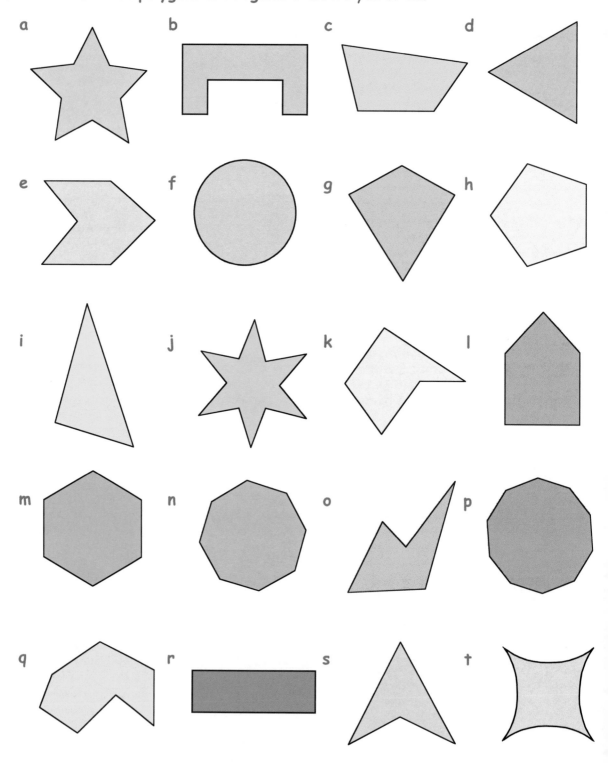

a   b   c   d

e   f   g   h

i   j   k   l

m   n   o   p

q   r   s   t

4. Imagine you were going to tile the walls of your bathroom.

Some of the shapes above would make good tiles, but some would not.

Write down which of them would work, which would not work, and write why you think they would not make good tiles.

The 3 Я's

1. Square, Rectangle, Rhombus, Kite, Parallelogram and Trapezium.

   How many of each can you see in this picture?

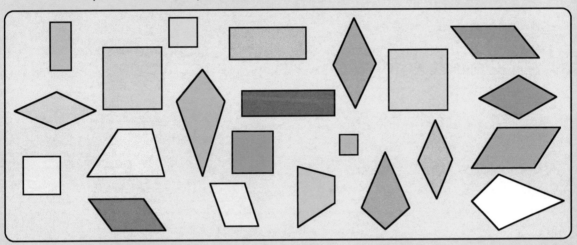

2. True (T) or False (F)?

   a   A kite is made up of 2 isosceles triangles.

   b   The opposite sides of a rhombus are parallel.

   c   A parallelogram has only 1 line of symmetry.

   d   A square fits into its outline 8 ways if you can turn it and rotate it.

   e   A rectangle has opposite sides equal and parallel.

3. Write down 3 ways in which a rhombus is different from a square.

4. Name the polygon which has 6 sides.

5. Which of these polygons are regular?

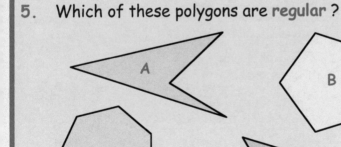
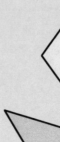
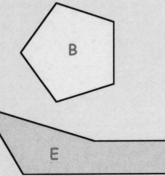
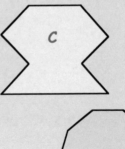

Money and Decimals

Be able to read and write money using decimals.

£1   can be written as   £1•00.

Remember this is called a decimal point.

93p   can be written as   £0•93.   (93p = $\frac{93}{100}$ of a £).

£6 and 52p can be written as   £6•52.

£74 and 37p can be written as   £74•37.

Always have **two** numbers to the right of the decimal point when working with **money.**

Exercise 1

1. Write these amounts using a **decimal point** :-   (37p = £0·37).

   a   95p   b   36p   c   120p   d   3p

   e   £3 and 99p   f   £15 and 10p   g   £145 and 80p   h   100p.

2. Write each of these without a **decimal point** :-

   a   £0·45   b   £0·72   c   £1·80   d   £8·21

   e   £10·50   f   £87·75   g   £1·00   h   £0·04.

Ninety four pence can be written as **94p** or **£0 · 94**

3. Write each amount in **two ways** (as above) :-

   a   seventy one pence   b   twenty two pence

   c   sixty pence   d   thirty pence

   e   one pound and ninety pence   f   sixteen pounds and five pence.

4. Write down the amount of money for each of these, using a decimal point :-

a

b

c

d

e

f

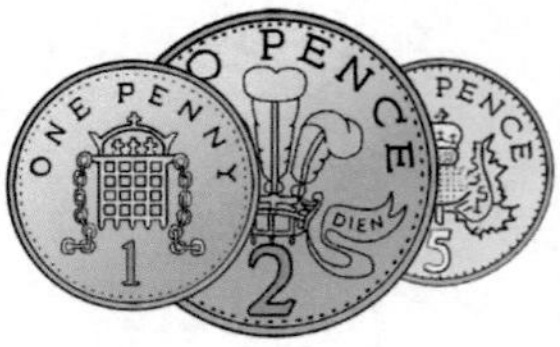

g

h

i

j

k

l

Adding and Subtracting Money with Decimals

Be able to add or subtract money in decimal form.

When you add or subtract money, you MUST line up the **decimal points**.

Examples :-   Addition

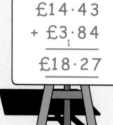

£14·43
+ £3·84
———
£18·27

Subtraction

£9·38
- £5·49
———
£3·89

Exercise 2

1.   Copy and complete :-

a   £3·25
      + £2·54
      ———

b   £6·53
      + £0·24
      ———

c   £29·35
      + £13·46
      ———

d   £6·72
      + £4·84
      ———

e   £7·74
      - £3·42
      ———

f   £19·45
      - £ 2·65
      ———

g   £61·28
      - £23·33
      ———

h   £118·43
      - £7·25
      ———

i   £215·98
      - £ 14·77
      ———

j   £129·43
      - £118·28
      ———

k   £102·25
      - £ 89·79
      ———

l   £49·67
      - £ 19·83
      ———

m   £84·49
      + £13·93
      ———

n   £618·13
      - £111·62
      ———

o   £202·24
      + £170·79
      ———

p   £140·49
      + £30·92
      ———

q   £138·32
      - £109·60
      ———

r   £812·54
      + £713·79
      ———

2. Set down these additions and subtractions in the same way as
    Question 1 and work out the answers :-

    a   £5·25 + £4·54   b   £19·57 – £7·26   c   £45·84 + £23·19

    d   £29·42 – £17·54   e   £18 + £5·42   f   £30 – £17·17

    g   £108 + £14·98   h   £85 – £61·98   i   £110·56 + £32·04

    j   £145 – £76·09   k   £989·94 + £9·99   l   £1018·44 – £978·35.

    m   £0·76 – 24p   n   £40·45 – 88p   o   £11·62 – 83p.

3. a   Frank has £12·74. His dad gives him £10·25.

        How much does Frank have now ?

    b      Jo spent £18·26 in a chemist shop
                               and £9·65 in a newspaper shop.

                               How much did Jo spend in **total** ?

    c   Li bought a blouse for £32·16 and a skirt for £18·86.

        How much did Li spend **altogether** ?

    d   Louise had £112·47. She won £78·75 in the lottery.

        How much did Louise then have **in total** ?

    e      Kate saved £135·75 last month.

                               This month she saved £87·75.

                               How much **more** had she saved last month ?

    f   Zara spent £135·86 from her £320 savings.

        How much did she have left ?

    g   Phillip has saved £123·81 in coins.

        On the way to the bank he lost 97p.

        How much could he put in the bank ?

Revisit - Review - Revise

1. Write each of these amounts using a decimal point :-

   a

   b

   c  d  e

2. Find:-

   a £33·34
      + £ 12·42

   b £117·47
      – £54·25

   c £92·47
      – £ 9·76

   d £18·73 – £14·87   e £143·81 + £116·97   f £564·17 – £74·83.

3. a Ellie had £44·62 in her piggy bank.

      She then put in another £12·78.

      How much did she have then ?

   b Ali spent £4·85 and gave a £10 note. How much change did she get ?

   c Jake got £13·45 change from his £20 note. How much had he spent ?

   d Michael gave the shopkeeper three £20 notes.

      He had bought two tops at £12·75 each and
      a football for £25·49.

      How much change should he have received ?

Time   Revision

Exercise 1

1. a   How many minutes are there in one hour ?

   b   How many seconds are there in one minute ?

   c   How many days are there in a leap year ?

2. Write down the time on each digital clock, in words :-

   a      b      c

3. Write down the time on each clock in 2 ways :-
   (*e.g. quarter to ten in the morning and 9:45 am*)

   a      b      c

   just started school   just home from school   asleep

4. Write down how many days there are in :-

   a   March   b   November   c   October.

5. Write each date using 6 digits :-

   a   8th May 2016   b   April tenth 2010   c   Christmas day 2020.

6. How many days are there between 20th May and 3rd June ?
   (Do **not** include the given dates).

Changing Units of Time

Be able to change basic units of time.

Remember - there are :-

60 minutes in an hour

60 seconds in a minute

24 hours in a day

7 days in a week.

When changing **seconds** to **minutes and seconds** it is easier to think in 60's.

Example :-   140 seconds = 60 secs + 60 secs + 20 secs = **2 mins 20 secs.**
                                    (1 min)   (1 min)

Exercise 2

1.   A tenor recorded a song lasting 105 seconds for an advert on TV.

     Write this time in **minutes** and **seconds**.

2.   Change each of these to **minutes** and **seconds** :-

a 90 secs	b 148 secs	c 220 secs
d 420 secs	e 335 secs	f 297 secs
g 600 secs	h 1230 secs	i 6000 secs.

3.   Change each of these to **hours** and **minutes** :-
     (*Same process as question 1.*)

a 85 mins	b 125 mins	c 245 mins
d 600 mins	e 1810 mins	f 9000 mins.

4.   Change from **minutes and seconds** to **seconds** :-

     a   8 mins and 20 secs b   9 mins & 45 secs   c   10 mins & 50 secs.

5.   Change from **hours and minutes** to **minutes** :-

     a   3 hrs and 10 mins   b   7 hrs & 30 mins   c   8 hrs & 50 mins.

6. How many months are there in :-

   a   2 years   b   3 years   c   6 years   d   10 years ?

7. How many days are there in :-

   a   5 weeks   b   8 weeks   c   20 weeks   d   a fortnight ?

8. a   Tam sang 3 songs in his spot on the "England's Got Talent" audition.

   "With You" - 3 mins 45 secs,   "Be Mine" - 2 mins 50 secs, and
   "Rainbow Boy" - 3 mins 25 secs.

   How many seconds did his songs last **altogether** ?

   b   Alicia has 45 days to pay her tax bill.

   How many **full weeks** does she have left to pay ?

   c   How many minutes are there in one weekend ?

   d   How many full months have you been alive ?

Adding

```
    5 mins   40 secs
  + 3 mins   50 secs
         1
    9 mins   30 secs
```
90 secs = 1 min 30 secs

Subtracting

```
         7    60 +
    8 mins   20 secs
  - 5 mins   50 secs
    2 mins   30 secs
```
60 + 20 - 50 = 30 secs

Remember :-

1 hour = 60 minutes
1 minute = 60 seconds

---

9. Copy and complete each of these :-

   a   4 mins 20 secs   b   4 mins 30 secs   c   8 mins 45 secs
         + 3 mins 35 secs   + 2 mins 50 secs   + 3 mins 55 secs

   d   7 mins 45 secs   e   7 mins 05 secs   f   7 mins 40 secs
         - 4 mins 30 secs   - 1 min   55 secs   - 6 mins 50 secs

   g   3 hrs   55 mins   h   9 hrs   15 mins   i   17 hrs 20 mins
         - 2 hrs   20 mins   - 4 hrs   20 mins   -   9 hrs 55 mins

Be able to read a stopwatch and time events.

This stopwatch shows the time in minutes and seconds.

The time shown is
4 minutes 13·07 seconds.

Exercise 3

1. State the times which are shown on the following stopwatches :–

   a  b  c  d  e

2. Here are the times for the first 6 runners to finish a 400 metre race :–

Samson - 45·27 secs	Thomson - 46·36 secs	McGovern - 44·78 secs
Murray - 46·45 secs	Goodwin - 45·08 secs	Van Zanten - 46·09 secs

   List the 6 runners in order, **winner first**.

3. Here are the individual times for each of the four runners for a top USA team in the 4 by 400 metre relay race in an event in Germany.

Morry - 44·61 secs,	Johnstone - 43·28 secs,
Watt - 42·94 secs,	Reynold - 43·78 secs

   Calculate the **total** time they took for the race, in **minutes and seconds**.

4. Here are the times for the four British runners :–

Steel - 44·59 secs,	Tobine - 43·76 secs,
Breingan - 43·1 secs,	Ronson - 43·69 secs

   a Calculate the total time the British team took.

   b Which team was faster ?   c How much faster ?

Revisit - Review - Revise

1. How many :-

    a   minutes in 3 hours   b   seconds in ten minutes

    c   days in a leap year   d   weeks in a year ?

2. How many days are there in :-

    a   November   b   April   c   October ?

3. How many hours are there in one week ?

4. Change each of these to minutes and seconds :-

    a   140 secs   b   345 secs   c   700 secs.

5. Change each of these to hours and minutes :-

    a   75 mins   b   165 mins   c   451 mins.

6. Change each of these from minutes and seconds to seconds :-

    a   4 mins 10 secs   b   10 mins 50 secs   c   8 mins 12 secs.

7. Change each of these from hours and minutes to minutes :-

    a   2 hrs 5 mins   b   9 hrs 25 mins   c   4 hrs 3 mins.

8. Copy and complete :-

    a   4 mins 20 secs   b   4 mins 30 secs   c   8 hrs 45 mins
        + 3 mins 35 secs   – 2 mins 15 secs   – 3 hrs 55 mins

9. Write these in order, shortest time first :-

       1·2 secs,   0·7 secs,   1·09 secs,   1·31 secs,   2 secs.

Multiplication & Division

Be able to multiply by 10, 100 and 1000 quickly.

Multiplication by 10, 100 (and 1000)

Examples :-

32	601	274	98
× 10	× 10	× 100	× 1000
320	6010	27 400	98 000

When you multiply a number, like **89**, by **10** (or **100** or **1000**), you will find that all the figures move 1, (or 2 or 3) places to the left of their place value

=> **890** (or **8900** or **89 000**)

Examples :-

46 × 10 = 460

10 × 258 = 2580

6506 × 100 = 650 600

1000 × 57 = 57 000

Exercise 1

1. Write down the answers to the following :-

a 15 × 10   b 45 × 10   c 56 × 10   d 10 × 200

e 10 × 625   f 718 × 10   g 10 × 400   h 10 × 790.

2. Write down the answers to the following :-

a 5 × 100   b 7 × 100   c 100 × 15   d 100 × 70

e 82 × 100   f 100 × 20   g 100 × 86   h 90 × 100.

3. Write down the answers to these :-

a 6 × 1000   b 3 × 1000   c 7 × 1000   d 1000 × 9.

4. A bar of chocolate contains 8 squares.

   How many squares are there in :-

   a 10 bars   b 100 bars   c 1000 bars ?

Division by 10, 100 (and 1000)

Be able to divide by 10, 100 and 1000 quickly.

Examples :-

$$\frac{3\,4}{10\,)\,3\,4\,\cancel{0}}$$

$$\frac{5\,0\,7}{10\,)\,5\,0\,7\,\cancel{0}}$$

$$\frac{3\,6\,1}{10\,)\,3\,6\,1\,\cancel{0}}$$

$$\frac{8\,5}{100\,)\,8\,5\,\cancel{0}\,\cancel{0}}$$

$$\frac{7\,0}{100\,)\,7\,0\,\cancel{0}\,\cancel{0}}$$

$$\frac{6}{1000\,)\,6\,\cancel{0}\,\cancel{0}\,\cancel{0}}$$

When you divide a number like **75 000** by **10** (or **100** or **1000**) you will find that all the figures move 1 (or 2 or 3) places to the right of their place value
=> **7500** (or **750** or **75**).

Examples :-

$$380 \div 10 = 38$$

$$5300 \div 10 = 530$$

$$8200 \div 100 = 82$$

$$3\,000 \div 1000 = 3$$

Exercise 2

1. Write down the answers to the following :-

   a $250 \div 10$ b $370 \div 10$ c $3500 \div 10$ d $8970 \div 10$

   e $9000 \div 10$ f $2000 \div 10$ g $4000 \div 10$ h $2500 \div 10.$

2. Write down the answers to the following :-

   a $600 \div 100$ b $1200 \div 100$ c $4600 \div 100$ d $6500 \div 100$

   e $7000 \div 100$ f $3500 \div 100$ g $9800 \div 100$ h $5000 \div 100.$

3. Write down the answers to the following :-

   a $3000 \div 1000$ b $7000 \div 1000$ c $9000 \div 1000$ d $12\,000 \div 1000.$

4. A biscuit factory produces 6000 biscuits each hour.

   How many boxes will be needed to pack them if each box holds :-

   a   10 biscuits   b   100 biscuits   c   1000 biscuits ?

11 Times Table

You should now know the :-

2 **times** table,
through to the
10 **times** table.

The **11 times** table can be
found in a similar way.

a **Copy** and complete the
green list, showing
11 sets of 5 etc.

b Now **copy** and complete
the list in the blue box,
to get your 11 times table.

11 sets of 0 = 0	0 × 11 = 0
11 sets of 1 = 11	1 × 11 = 11
11 sets of 2 = 22	2 × 11 = 22
11 sets of 3 = 33	3 × 11 = 33
11 sets of 4 = 44	4 × 11 = 44
11 sets of 5 = ...	5 × 11 = ...
11 sets of 6 = ...	6 × 11 = ...
11 sets of .. = ...	.. × 11 = ...
11 sets of .. = ...	.. × 11 = ...
11 sets of .. = ...	.. × 11 = ...
11 sets of .. = ...	.. × 11 = ...
11 sets of 11 = ...	.. × 11 = ...
11 sets of 12 = ...	.. × 11 = ...

Can you see the simple pattern :- 0, 11, 22, 33, 44, 55, ... ?

Exercise 3

1. **Copy** and **complete** :-

a 4 × 11 =   b 11 × 5 =   c 11 × 2 =

d 3 × 11 =   e 11 × 6 =   f 7 × 11 =

g 11 × 12 =   h 8 × 11 =   i 11 × 9 =   .

2. What numbers are **missing** ?

a .... × 11 = 11   b .... × 11 = 55   c .... × 11 = 66

d .... × 11 = 0   e .... × 11 = 88   f 11 × .... = 44

g .... × 11 = 110   h 11 × .... = 99   i .... × 11 = 121.

3. **a** A hospital ordered **8** boxes of bandages.

There are **11** bandages in each box.

How many bandages will the hospital have ?

b  Joe planted **10** rows of daffodils in his garden.

He placed **11** in each row.

How many daffodils did he have altogether ?

c There are **11** rolchies in a packet.

Jane buys **6** packets.

How many rolchies will she have ?

d  **Eleven** people sponsored Charlene in a bike run.

They each gave **£5**.

How much did Charlene raise ?

e Each question in a science test is worth **3** marks.

Sammy got **11** questions correct.

How many marks did he get ?

f  A magazine was giving away **7** free vouchers.

Daisy bought **11** magazines !

How many vouchers did she get ?

g The swimming pool at my hotel is **12** metres long.

How far will I cover if I swim **11** lengths ?

h  A 3 course lunch at The Chung Palace costs **£11**.

Penny and her **10** friends went there for lunch.

What did it cost them ?

Dividing by 11

Dividing by 11, sometimes with a remainder.

Can you remember your 11 times table ?

1 x 11 = 11	2 x 11 = 22	3 x 11 = 33	4 x 11 = 44
5 x 11 = 55	6 x 11 = 66	7 x 11 = 77	8 x 11 = 88
9 x 11 = 99	10 x 11 = 110	11 x 11 = 121	12 x 11 = 132

Example 1 :-

    55 ÷ 11

55 ÷ 11 = **5**

from knowing
the 11 times table.

Example 2 :-

    80 ÷ 11

80 ÷ 11 = **7 r 3**

from knowing that
7 x 11 = 77

.... + 3 = 80

Exercise 4

1. Copy each of these and **complete** :-

   a   44 ÷ 11 = ...

   b   99 ÷ 11 = ...

   c   66 ÷ 11 = ...

   d   88 ÷ 11 = ...

   e   33 ÷ 11 = ...

   f   22 ÷ 11 = ...

   g   11 ÷ 11 = ...

   h   77 ÷ 11 = ...

   i   110 ÷ 11 = ...

   j   132 ÷ 11 = ...

   k   121 ÷ 11 = ...

   l   12 ÷ 11 = ...

   m   60 ÷ 11 = ...

   n   92 ÷ 11 = ...

   o   39 ÷ 11 = ...

   p   52 ÷ 11 = ...

   q   131 ÷ 11 = ...

   r   155 ÷ 11 = ...

2. Find the missing numbers :-

   a ◯ ÷ 11 = 7

   b ◯ ÷ 11 = 10

   c ◯ ÷ 11 = 2

   d ◯ ÷ 11 = 9

   e ◯ ÷ 11 = 12

   f ◯ ÷ 11 = 8.

3. a There are **33** monkeys in a zoo in **11** cages.

How many monkeys are in each cage ?

b  **66** boys and girls turned up to take part in a charity football tournament.

Each team had to have **11** players.

How many teams could be formed ?

c A baker has **110** rolls and **11** bags.

He puts the same number of rolls into each bag.

How many rolls per bag ?

d  There are **132** tyres on **11** similar trucks.

How many tyres are on each truck ?

e Freddie got **55** out of 60 in his maths test.

He got **11** questions correct.

(i) How many marks was each question worth ?

(ii) How many questions were in the test ?

f  There were **89** sheep in a field.

Ten more were put in and they were then split equally into **11** pens.

How many sheep were in each pen ?

g There are **16** children at a party.

5 of the children go home early.

The others share **22** packets of crisps.

How many packets do they receive each ?

12 Times Table

You should now know the :-

    2 **times** table,
    through to the
    11 **times** table.

The 12 **times** table can be found in a similar way.

a   **Copy** and complete the green list, showing 12 sets of 5 etc.

b   Now **copy** and complete the list in the blue box, to get your 12 times table.

12 sets of 0 = 0	0 x 12 = 0
12 sets of 1 = 12	1 x 12 = 12
12 sets of 2 = 24	2 x 12 = 24
12 sets of 3 = 36	3 x 12 = 36
12 sets of 4 = 48	4 x 12 = 48
12 sets of 5 = ...	5 x 12 = ...
12 sets of 6 = ...	6 x 12 = ...
12 sets of .. = ...	.. x 12 = ...
12 sets of .. = ...	.. x 12 = ...
12 sets of .. = ...	.. x 12 = ...
12 sets of .. = ...	.. x 12 = ...
12 sets of 11 = ...	.. x 12 = ...
12 sets of 12 = ...	.. x 12 = ...

Exercise 5

1.   **Copy** and **complete** :-

   a $3 \times 12 =$ b $6 \times 12 =$ c $2 \times 12 =$

   d $4 \times 12 =$ e $5 \times 12 =$ f $9 \times 12 =$

   g $11 \times 12 =$ h $12 \times 12 =$ i $7 \times 12 =$.

2.   What numbers are **missing** ?

   a $12 \times .... = 0$ b $12 \times .... = 60$ c $12 \times .... = 72$

   d $12 \times .... = 108$ e $.... \times 12 = 24$ f $12 \times .... = 84$

   g $12 \times .... = 144$ h $12 \times .... = 132$ i $.... \times 12 = 120$.

3.

a A roller coaster at an amusement park has **5** carriages.

Each carriage can hold **12** people.

How many people in total can the roller coaster take ?

b 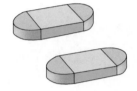 Miss Primm has **10** boxes of erasers.

Each box has **12** in it.

How many erasers has she altogether ?

c There are **4** men in a relay team.

Each man has to complete **12** laps.

Over how many laps is the race?

d  A village plans to plant **8** trees in each of its play areas.

It has **12** play areas.

How many trees are needed ?

e A pet store has **12** large cages with mice in them.

Each cage has **11** mice.

How many mice does the store have ?

f  An apartment building has **3** floors.

Each floor has **12** apartments on it.

How many apartments are in the building ?

g Archie bought **12** bags of potatoes, with **12** potatoes in each bag.

How many potatoes did Archie buy ?

h  A bottle of red wine costs **£9**.

What would I pay for a case of **12** bottles ?

Dividing by 12

Dividing by 12, sometimes with a remainder.

Have you learned your 12 times table ?

1 x 12 = 12	2 x 12 = 24	3 x 12 = 36	4 x 12 = 48
5 x 12 = 60	6 x 12 = 72	7 x 12 = 84	8 x 12 = 96
9 x 12 = 108	10 x 12 = 120	11 x 12 = 132	12 x 12 = 144

Example 1 :-

48 ÷ 12

48 ÷ 12 = **4**

from knowing the 12 times table.

Example 2 :-

41 ÷ 12

41 ÷ 12 = **3** R 5

from knowing that
3 x 12 = 36
.... + 5 = 41

Exercise 6

1. Copy each of these and **complete** :-

    a   60 ÷ 12 = ...

    b   24 ÷ 12 = ...

    c   72 ÷ 12 = ...

    d   96 ÷ 12 = ...

    e   36 ÷ 12 = ...

    f   108 ÷ 12 = ...

    g   12 ÷ 12 = ...

    h   120 ÷ 12 = ...

    i   144 ÷ 12 = ...

    j   132 ÷ 12 = ...

    k   84 ÷ 12 = ...

    l   14 ÷ 12 = ...

    m   61 ÷ 12 = ...

    n   89 ÷ 12 = ...

    o   116 ÷ 12 = ...

    p   46 ÷ 12 = ...

    q   40 ÷ 12 = ...

    r   131 ÷ 12 = ...

2. Find the missing numbers :-

    a   ◯ ÷ 12 = 4

    b   ◯ ÷ 12 = 7

    c   ◯ ÷ 12 = 9

    d   ◯ ÷ 12 = 10

    e   ◯ ÷ 12 = 12

    f   ◯ ÷ 12 = 8.

3. a   Nan bought **36** Christmas cards which came **12** to a box.

How many boxes did she buy ?

b   You used to get **12** old pennies for a shilling.

If I had **108** old pennies, how many shillings
would I have had ?

c   Eggs used to be bought by the dozen (**12**).

If a chef used **132** eggs, how many dozen was that ?

d    Lena was paid **£84** for working a **12** hour shift.

What did she get paid per hour ?

e   **12** children brought a total of **60** balls to play tennis.

If they each brought the same number, how many was that ?

f    A florist has **125** flowers to put into
bunches of **12**.

How many full bunches will she be able to make ?

g   Mr Thom has **100** pencils.

He throws out **4** that are broken and splits the
rest equally amongst **12** pencil tidies.

How many pencils are in one tidy ?

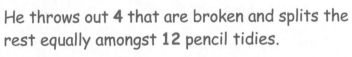

h   A waitress counted the number of plates in a restaurant.

She counted **136**.

She then put **8** brand new ones with these
and piled the plates into bundles of **12**.

How many bundles did she make?

1. Write down the answer to each of these :-

   a 23 × 10   b 250 × 10   c 80 × 100   d 36 × 100

   e 420 ÷ 10   f 6800 ÷ 100 g 5100 ÷ 10   h 5000 ÷ 1000

   i 8 × 11   j 11 × 12   k 12 × 4   l 8 × 12

   m 77 ÷ 11   n 121 ÷ 11   o 60 ÷ 12   p 144 ÷ 12.

2. Boxes of 100 light bulbs were on sale in an electrical store.

   In just one hour, 19 boxes were sold.

   How many bulbs was that ?

3. 8 football teams took part in an 11-a-side tournament.

   In round one, all the teams took part.

   How many players was that altogether ?

4.

   Tom buys 11 bags of sweets for his party.

   There are 10 sweets in each bag.

   If there are 5 friends coming to the party, how many sweets will they each get ?

5. Frank decides to save £10 every month for 3 years.

   a   How much will he have at the end of one year ?

   b   How much will he have at the end of 3 years ?

6. A group of 12 people spent £114 in total at the motor show.

   It was £6 for parking the minibus and the rest of the money was for entry into the show.

   How much did it cost for one ticket for the show ?

Chapter 19

Measure

Converting Units of Length

Be able to convert between different units of length.

There are 4 main units of length used in the **METRIC** system.

kilometre   millimetre
metre   centimetre

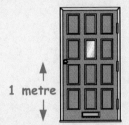

The metre

This is the standard unit of length - it is about the distance from the ground to the handle of a door in your house.

1 metre

The centimetre

This is the metre divided into 100 parts.
It is about the width of your pinky nail.

1 cm

1 metre

The millimetre

This is the centimetre divided into 10 parts.
It is about the width of a thin needle.

1 cm

The kilometre

This is equal to 1000 metres.
It is about the distance walking 3 times around a football pitch.

Exercise 1

1. How many :-

   a   centimetres are there in 1 metre

   b   metres are there in 1 kilometre

   c   millimetres are there in 1 centimetre

   d   millimetres are there in 1 metre

   e   centimetres are there in 1 kilometre

   f   millimetres are there in 1 kilometre ?

640 km

2. Since **1 cm = 10 mm**, how many millimetres are there in :-

a   4 cm   b   7 cm   c   10 cm   d   25 cm

e   70 cm   f   200 cm   g   3 cm 5 mm   h   2 cm 9 mm

i   9 cm 6 mm   j   10 cm 5 mm   k   15 cm 1 mm   l   half a cm ?

3. Since **10 mm = 1 cm**, how many centimetres are equal to :-

a   30 mm   b   50 mm   c   90 mm   d   110 mm

e   400 mm   f   330 mm   g   700 mm   h   890 mm

i   1000 mm   j   3000 mm   k   5500 mm   l   5 mm ?

4. Since **1 m = 100 cm**, how many centimetres are there in :-

a   4 m   b   7 m   c   9 m   d   10 m

e   45 m   f   57 m   g   3 m 5 cm   h   half of a metre

i   6 m 20 cm   j   25 m 90 cm   k   100 m   l   quarter of a metre

5. Remember, **100 cm = 1 m**. How many metres are there in :-

a   200 cm   b   600 cm   c   900 cm   d   1200 cm

e   3500 cm   f   8700 cm   g   9200 cm   h   10 000 cm

i   4000 cm   j   6200 cm   k   12 000 cm   l   50 cm ?

6. **1 km = 1000 m.** Write down how many metres there are in :-

a   4 km   b   9 km   c   10 km   d   1 km 500 m

e   2 km 700 m   f   4 km 250 m   g   6 km 90 m   h   half a kilometre.

7. **1000 m = 1 km.** Write as kilometres or as kilometres and metres :-

a   3000 m   b   7000 m   c   10 000 m   d   5000 m

e   2850 m   f   4820 m   g   8790 m   h   500 m.

8. Put these four lengths in order, **largest** first :-

82 mm - 8 cm 4 mm - 8 cm - 8 cm 1 mm.

Converting Units of Volume

Be able to convert between different units of volume.

Litres and Millilitres.

Since there are 1000 ml in 1 litre, to change from one to the other **multiply** or **divide** the given amount by **1000**.

litres —> (x 1000) —> millilitres   millilitres —> (÷ 1000) —> litres

Example 1 :-

9 litres 200 ml becomes

(9 x **1000** + 200) ml

= (9000 + 200) ml

= 9200 ml

Example 2 :-

8300 ml becomes

(8300 ÷ **1000**) =

(8 litres remainder 300)

= 8 litres 300 ml

Example 3 :-

$6\frac{1}{4}$ litres becomes

6 x **1000** + (1000 ÷ 4) ml

= (6000 + 250) ml

= 6250 ml.

Exercise 2

1. Change the following to millilitres :-

   a   5 litres   b   8 litres   c   1 litre 500 ml

   d   3 litres 200 ml   e   7 litres 250 ml   f   8 litres 840 ml

   g   1 litre 10 ml   h   4 litres 50 ml   i   7 litres 75 ml

   j   2 litres 4 ml   k   half a litre   l $3\frac{1}{2}$ litres.

2. The volumes shown below are in millilitres.

   Change them to **litres** – OR – to **litres AND ml** :-

   a   3000 ml   b   5000 ml   c   9000 ml

   d   6000 ml   e   2000 ml   f   500 ml

   g   1500 ml   h   2800 ml   i   3400 ml

   j   5430 ml   k   6870 ml   l   2020 ml.

3. Put these four volumes in order, **smallest** first :-

   3 litres 200 ml - 3100 ml - 3 litres 20 ml - 3010 ml.

Converting Units of Weight

Be able to convert between different units of weight.

The Kilogram and the Gram.

A gram is a small unit used to weigh objects.

It indicates how heavy the object is.

A packet of crisps weighs about 30 grams.

A kilogram is made up of 1000 grams.

Scales are used to weigh objects.

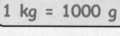

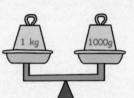

1 kg = 1000 g

1 cm
1 cm
1 cm

If you fill a hollow cube of side 1 centimetre with water, it will weigh 1 gram.

Examples :-

3 kg	4750 g	2 kg 30 g	6000 g
= 3 x 1000 g	= (4750 ÷ 1000) g	= (2000 + 30) g	= (6000 ÷ 1000) g
= 3000 g	= 4 kg 750 g	= 2030 g	= 6 kg

Exercise 3

1. Write these weights in **grams** :-

    a   4 kg   b   9 kg   c   7 kg

    d   5 kg   e   10 kg   f   4 kg 500 g

    g   1 kg 600 g   h   6 kg 350 g   i   8 kg 910 g

    j   4 kg 725 g   k   5 kg 37 g   l   9 kg 66 g

    m   6 kg 90 g   n   10 kg 3 g   o   4 kg 4 g.

2. The weights shown below are in grams.

    Change them to **kilograms** - OR - to kilograms AND grams :-

    a   5000 g   b   8000 g   c   7000 g

    d   4000 g   e   9000 g   f   10000 g

    g   3200 g   h   8900 g   i   7400 g

    j   8540 g   k   9560 g   l   4050 g

    m   8003 g   n   5010 g   o   1018 g.

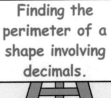

Finding the perimeter of a shape involving decimals.

We have already learned that the perimeter of a shape is the **total distance** around its outside.

We now look at examples where the shape's lengths are in decimal form.

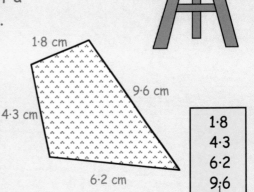

1·8 cm

9·6 cm

4·3 cm

6·2 cm

Example :- Find the perimeter of this shape.

Perimeter = (1·8 + 4·3 + 6·2 + 9·6) cm

= **21·9 cm**

```
  1·8
  4·3
  6·2
  9ᵢ6
 ____
 21·9
```

Exercise 4

1. By adding the sides, find the perimeter of each of these shapes :-

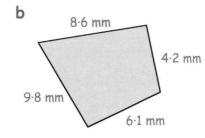

a

4·8 cm   2·5 cm

5·6 cm

b

8·6 mm

4·2 mm

9·8 mm

6·1 mm

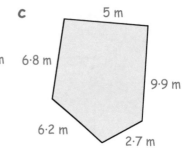

c

5 m

6·8 m

9·9 m

6·2 m

2·7 m

2. Work out the perimeter of each of these squares and rectangles :-

a

5·2 cm   square

b

3·9 cm

7·5 cm

c

6·6 cm

2·8 cm

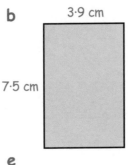

d

12·5 cm

2·5 cm

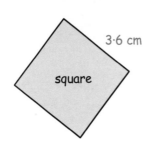

e

3·6 cm

square

1·2 cm

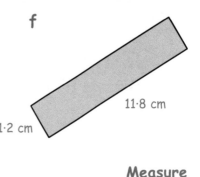

f

11·8 cm

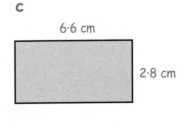

3. Calculate the length of the missing side in each of these figures :-

a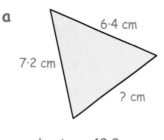
6·4 cm
7·2 cm
? cm
perimeter = 19·2 cm

b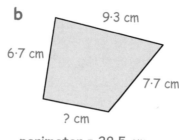
9·3 cm
6·7 cm
7·7 cm
? cm
perimeter = 28·5 cm

c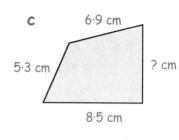
6·9 cm
5·3 cm
? cm
8·5 cm
perimeter = 28·2 cm

4. a A square has a **perimeter** of **28·4 cm.**

What is the length of one side ?

b A rectangle has length **12·5 cm** and
perimeter of **38 cm.**

Calculate the width of the rectangle.

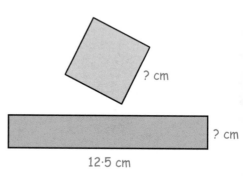
? cm
? cm
12·5 cm

5. Calculate the size of the missing side in each of these rectangles :-

a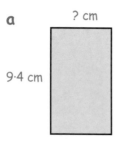
? cm
9·4 cm
perimeter = 26 cm

b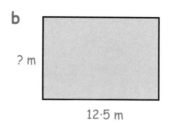
? m
12·5 m
perimeter = 43·6 m

c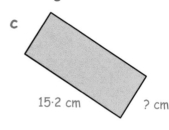
15·2 cm
? cm
perimeter = 40 cm

6. Another way to find the **perimeter of a rectangle** is to use the rule :-

"**Double its length, double its width** and **add your two answers**".

Example :- This rectangle's perimeter would be :-

2 x 2·1 + 2 x 1·5 = 4·2 + 3 = 7·2 cm.

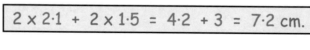
1·5 cm
2·1 cm

10·3 cm
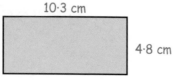
4·8 cm

Use this rule to find the perimeter
of this rectangle.

An Introduction to Area

The **area** of a shape is defined as the ...

AMOUNT OF SPACE IT COVERS.

A square, measuring 1 cm by 1 cm is said to have an

area of **1 square centimetre**.

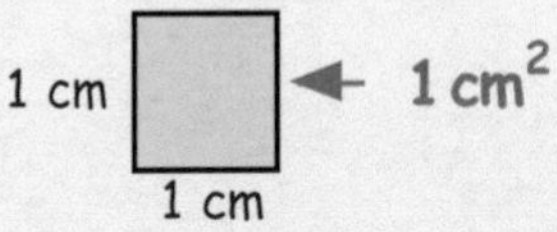

This is written as :- $1\ cm^2$

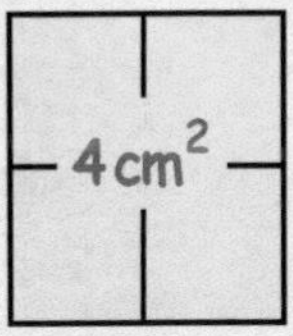

1 cm   ← $1\ cm^2$
1 cm

This shape has **4** similar squares. It has an **area** of **4 cm²**.

$4\,cm^2$

Exercise 5

1. Write down the area (..... cm²) of this shape.

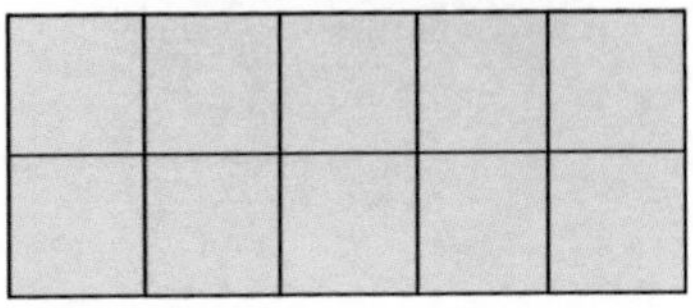

2. Write down the area (..... cm²) of each shape below :-

a

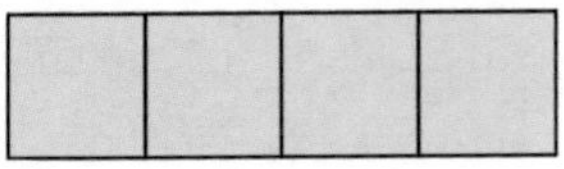

b

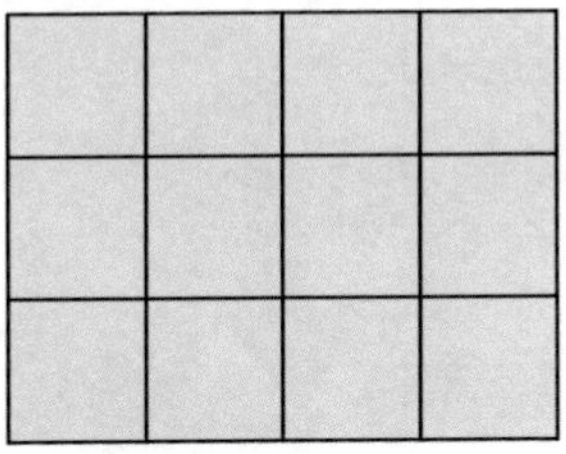

c

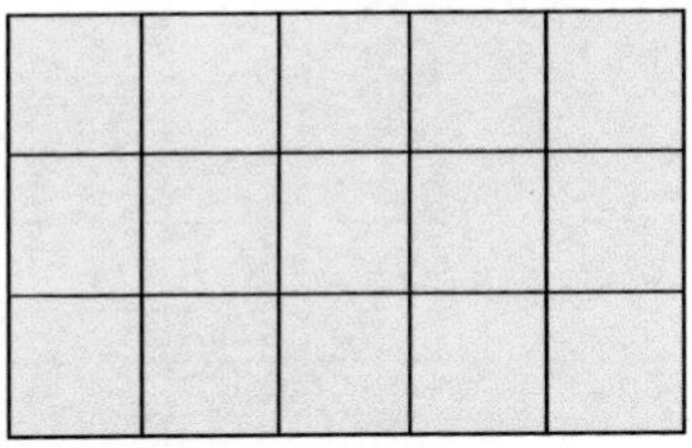

d

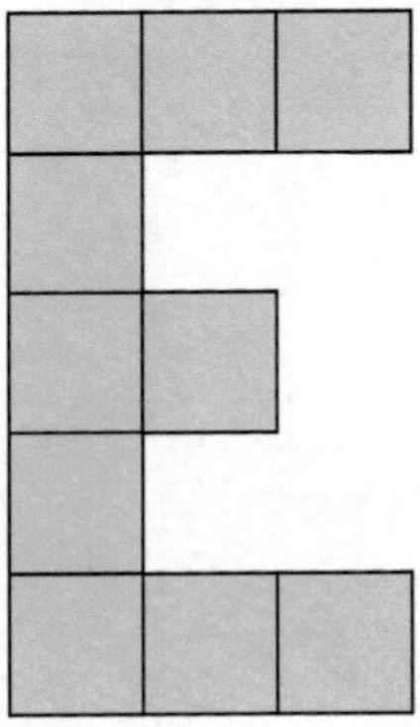

e

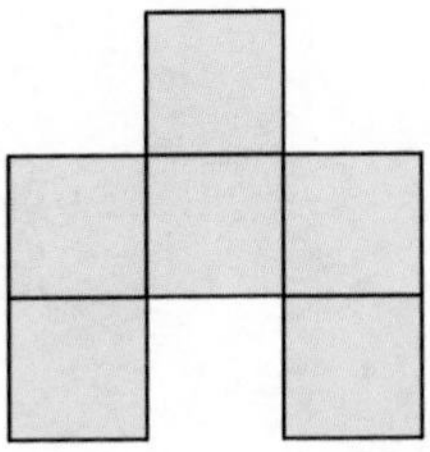

f

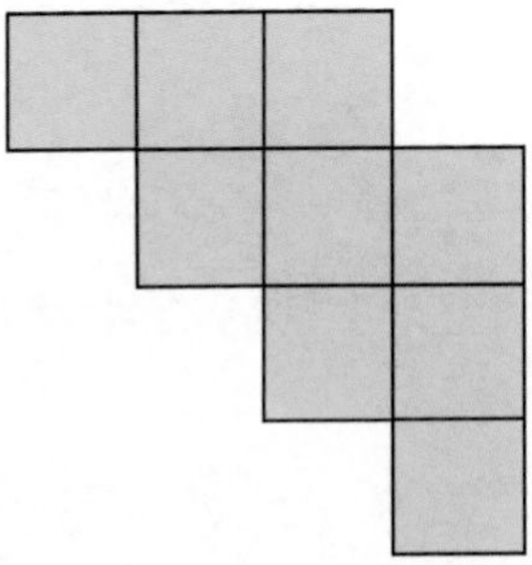

g

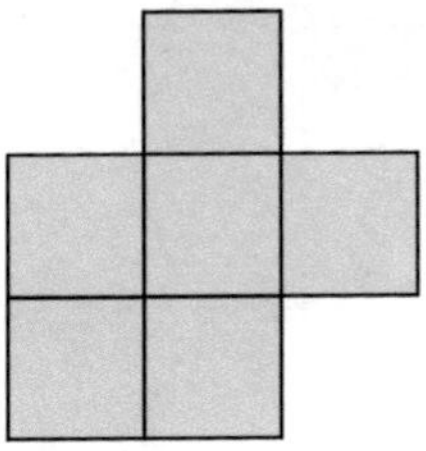

h

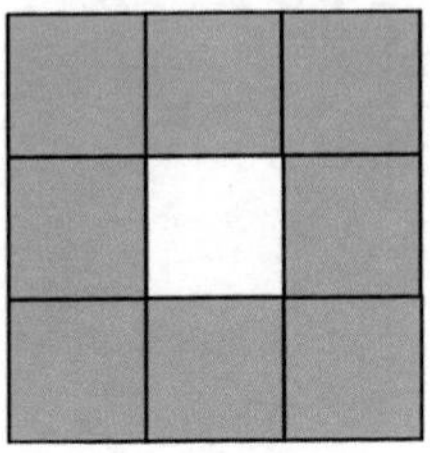

i

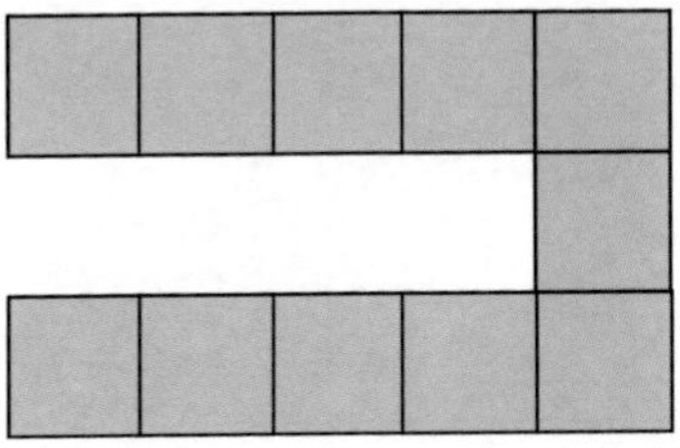

3. Write down the area (....cm^2) of each shape below :-

a

b

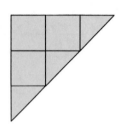

c

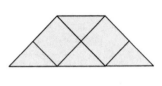

d

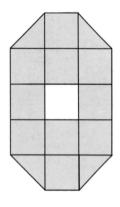

e

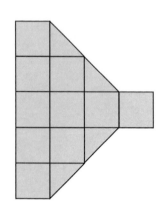

f

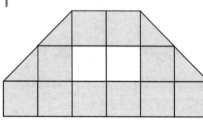

g

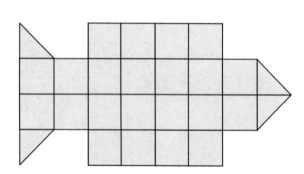

h

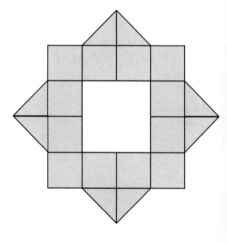

i

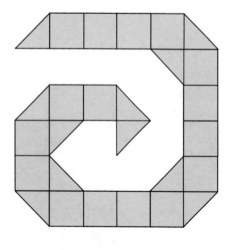

j

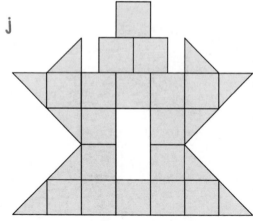

Estimating Area

Be able to estimate the area of a shape by counting square centimetres.

It is possible to **estimate** the area of a shape which is not made of squares and half squares.

Example :- To find the **area** of this blue shape :-

- Begin by counting all the **whole squares**.
- **Add** on any bits that are **more than** $\frac{1}{2}$ covered.
- **Ignore** any bits that are **less than** $\frac{1}{2}$ covered.

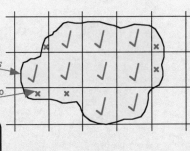

An **estimate** for the **area** of this shape is **9 cm²**.

1. **Estimate** the area (....cm²) of the shape opposite :-

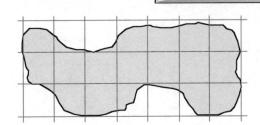

2. **Estimate** the area of each of these :-

a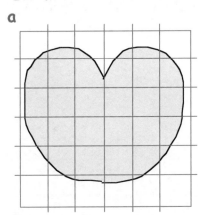

b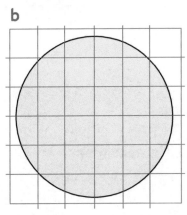

c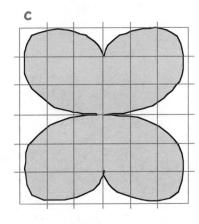

d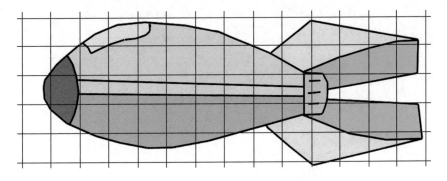

1.   Change :-

   a   5 cm to mm   b   6 cm 2 mm to mm   c   600 mm to cm

   d   28 mm to cm & mm   e   8 m to cm   f   7m 25 cm to cm

   g   400 cm to m   h   1250 cm to m & cm   i   3 km to m

   j   8 km 250 m to m   k   6000 m to km   l   5210 m to km & m.

2.   Change :-

   a   7 litres to ml   b   1 litre 100 ml to ml   c   2 litres 20 ml to ml

   d   6000 ml to litres   e   2500 ml to L & ml   f   8235 ml to L & ml.

3.   Change :-

   a   9 kg to g   b   2 kg 400 g to g   c   4 kg 50 g to g

   d   7000 g to kg   e   4800 g to kg & g   f   1234 g to kg & g.

4.   Find the perimeter of the square and the rectangle.

   a   b

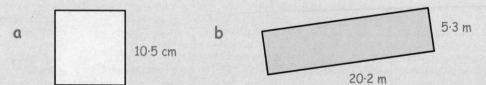

   10·5 cm   5·3 m

                            20·2 m

5.   Write down the area of this shape in cm² .

6.

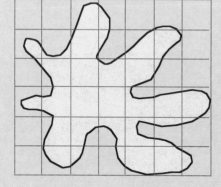

   Estimate the area of this shape in cm².

   *If more than half a box is
   covered, count it as 1 cm².

   If not, don't count it !

Chapter 20

Fractions

Fractions   Revision

Be able to identify a fraction.

Earlier you learned how to identify fractions.

Examples :-

This shape shows 3 out of 4 equal parts are **green**.

This shape shows 3 out of 5 equal parts are **purple**.

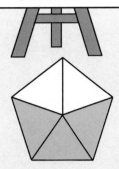

$\frac{3}{4}$ of this shape is **green**.

$\frac{1}{4}$ of this shape is **not green**.

$\frac{3}{5}$ of this shape is **purple**.

$\frac{2}{5}$ of this shape is **not purple**.

| Exercise 1 | *This exercise may be done orally.*

1.   a   What fraction of this circle is coloured **red** ?

     b   What fraction is not red ?

2.   What fraction of each shape is the **red** bit ?

a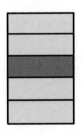
b
c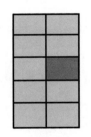
d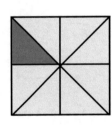

e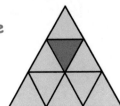
f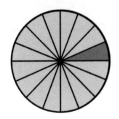
g
h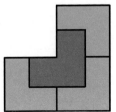

3.   Write down for each shape in Question **2** the fraction **not red**.

Two fractions might look different because they have different **numerators** (*top of the fraction*) and different **denominators** (*bottom of the fraction*) but they might still represent the same number.

Look at these diagrams representing fractions :-

fig. 1

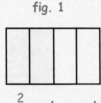

$\frac{2}{4}$ coloured

fig. 2

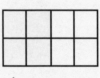

$\frac{4}{8}$ coloured

fig. 3

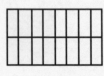

$\frac{8}{16}$ coloured

In each shape $\frac{1}{2}$ has been coloured.   This means $\frac{1}{2}$ = $\frac{2}{4}$ = $\frac{4}{8}$ = $\frac{8}{16}$.

These are called **equivalent** fractions.   (*Equivalent means the same as*).

Exercise 2

1. Copy the following and write down underneath each figure what **fraction** is shaded.

$\frac{1}{2}$ $\frac{?}{?}$ $\frac{?}{15}$ $\frac{?}{6}$ $\frac{?}{?}$ $\frac{?}{9}$

a   From the pictures you can see another **fraction** equal to $\frac{1}{2}$. ($\frac{1}{2}$ = $\frac{?}{?}$).

b   The second and last diagrams show that $\frac{1}{3}$ is the same as $\frac{?}{?}$.

c   The third and the fifth diagram show that $\frac{?}{15}$ is the same as $\frac{?}{?}$.

It is possible to find a fraction **equivalent** to $\frac{1}{4}$ by simply "multiplying the numerator and the denominator by the same number".

=> $\frac{1}{4}$ becomes $\dfrac{1 \times 5}{4 \times 5} = \dfrac{5}{20}$ numerator x 5
   denominator x 5

2. a Multiply the top and the bottom of $\frac{1}{5}$ by **2** to create a new fraction. What is it ?

   b Multiply the top and the bottom of $\frac{1}{5}$ by **3** to create a new fraction. What is it ?

   c Multiply the top and the bottom of $\frac{1}{5}$ by **10** to create a new fraction. What is it ?

3. a Multiply the top and the bottom of $\frac{2}{3}$ by **2** to create a new fraction. What is it ?

   b Multiply the top and the bottom of $\frac{2}{3}$ by **3** to form a new fraction. What is it ?

   c Find **four** more fractions equivalent to $\frac{2}{3}$.

4. Multiply the top and bottom of each fraction by 2 to create a new fraction **equivalent** to the one given :-

   a $\frac{1}{2}$ b $\frac{2}{5}$ c $\frac{3}{7}$ d $\frac{5}{8}$

   e $\frac{9}{10}$ f $\frac{11}{15}$ g $\frac{7}{12}$ h $\frac{11}{50}$.

5. Repeat Question **4**, but multiply the top and bottom of each fraction by 3.

6. Multiply the top and bottom of each fraction by a number of your own choice to create a new fraction **equivalent** to the one given :-

   a $\frac{2}{3}$ b $\frac{5}{7}$ c $\frac{7}{9}$ d $\frac{3}{8}$.

We can **SIMPLIFY** fractions (like $\frac{15}{18}$) by "dividing" top and bottom by a number.

=> $\boxed{\frac{15}{18} \text{ becomes } \frac{15 \div 3}{18 \div 3} = \frac{5}{6}}$ (*This cannot be **simplified** any further*).

* *This is where knowing all your **tables** will really help.*

7. Divide the top line and bottom line of each fraction by 2, to simplify :-

a $\frac{6 \div 2}{8 \div 2}$ b $\frac{2}{12}$ c $\frac{10}{14}$ d $\frac{6}{16}$

e $\frac{18}{20}$ f $\frac{22}{32}$ g $\frac{44}{54}$ h $\frac{18}{92}$.

8. Divide the top line and bottom line of each fraction by 3, to simplify :-

a $\frac{3 \div 3}{6 \div 3}$ b $\frac{6}{9}$ c $\frac{9}{12}$ d $\frac{9}{15}$

e $\frac{18}{21}$ f $\frac{15}{27}$ g $\frac{33}{66}$ h $\frac{150}{450}$.

9. For each of the following fractions, divide the numerator and the denominator by a number to **simplify** the fraction :-
(*Check that your answer can't be simplified further*).

a $\frac{15}{18}$ b $\frac{4}{10}$ c $\frac{6}{18}$ d $\frac{7}{14}$

e $\frac{10}{25}$ f $\frac{20}{30}$ g $\frac{12}{16}$ h $\frac{10}{15}$

i $\frac{9}{21}$ j $\frac{20}{24}$ k $\frac{12}{15}$ l $\frac{18}{20}$

m $\frac{30}{40}$ n $\frac{10}{100}$ o $\frac{40}{60}$ p $\frac{25}{100}$

q $\frac{6}{60}$ r $\frac{5}{100}$ s $\frac{150}{500}$ t $\frac{240}{360}$.

10. Simplify as far as possible :-

a $\frac{22}{33}$ b $\frac{26}{39}$ c $\frac{30}{45}$ d $\frac{360}{480}$ e $\frac{63}{99}$ f $\frac{4500}{6000}$.

Fractions of a Quantity (basic)

Be able to find a basic fraction of a number.

To find $\frac{1}{4}$ of something, you **divide** by 4.

To find $\frac{1}{6}$, **divide** by 6.

To find $\frac{1}{10}$, **divide** by 10.

Examples :-

Find :- a $\frac{1}{4}$ of 20   b $\frac{1}{6}$ of 18   c $\frac{1}{10}$ of 80

$$20 \div 4$$
$$= 5$$

$$18 \div 6$$
$$= 3$$

$$80 \div 10$$
$$= 8$$

Exercise 3

1. Find :-

    a $\frac{1}{3}$ of 15   b $\frac{1}{2}$ of 40   c $\frac{1}{4}$ of 24

    d $\frac{1}{5}$ of 30   e $\frac{1}{3}$ of 21   f $\frac{1}{5}$ of 60

    g $\frac{1}{4}$ of 60   h $\frac{1}{3}$ of 48   i $\frac{1}{4}$ of 100

    j $\frac{1}{3}$ of 120   k $\frac{1}{5}$ of 300   l $\frac{1}{2}$ of 150.

2. Find :-

    a $\frac{1}{7}$ of 21   b $\frac{1}{8}$ of 48   c $\frac{1}{9}$ of 72

    d $\frac{1}{8}$ of 72   e $\frac{1}{6}$ of 84   f $\frac{1}{10}$ of 340

    g $\frac{1}{8}$ of 400   h $\frac{1}{9}$ of 810   i $\frac{1}{7}$ of 140.

3. **a** There are 36 desks in a classroom.

$\frac{1}{4}$ of them are in need of repair.

How many desks need repaired ?

b  A cafe served 42 packs of sandwiches.

$\frac{1}{3}$ of the packs were BLT's.

How many BLT packs were sold ?

c Last week, Citreault produced 60 new cars.

$\frac{1}{5}$ of the cars were exported to France.

How many cars went to France ?

d There are 48 jelly beans in a jar.

$\frac{1}{6}$ of them are red.

How many red jelly beans are there ?

e A tank in a pet shop held 40 tropical fish.

$\frac{1}{8}$ of them were goldfish.

(i) How many goldfish were there in the tank ?

(ii) How many of the fish were **not** goldfish ?

f  $\frac{1}{10}$ of the trees in an orchard were pear

trees and $\frac{1}{5}$ of them were apple.

If there were 60 trees altogether,

(i) how many pear trees were there

(ii) how many apples trees ?

4. Jerry was on a 60 kilometre cycling trip for charity.

He got a puncture **one third** of the way into the trip.

a How far had Jerry cycled before the puncture ?

b How many kilometres had he still to go ?

Fractions of a Quantity

Be able to find any fraction of a quantity.

To find $\frac{2}{3}$ of a number (like 15), you do it **using 2 steps**.

Step 1 :- Find $\frac{1}{3}$ of 15 first (÷ 3) => $\frac{1}{3}$ of 15 = 15 ÷ 3 = **5**

Step 2 :- Now find $\frac{2}{3}$ of 15 by (x 2) => $\frac{2}{3}$ of 15 = **5 x 2 = 10**

Set the working down as follows :-

$\frac{3}{5}$ of 25 => (25 ÷ 5) x 3 = 5 x 3 = **15.**

$\frac{2}{7}$ of 35 => (35 ÷ 7) x 3 = 5 x 2 = **10.**

$\frac{7}{10}$ of 60 => (60 ÷ 10) x 7 = 6 x 7 = **42.**

Rule :-

To find a fraction, like $\frac{5}{8}$ of something,

=> "divide by the denominator" (8)

=> then "multiply by the numerator" (5)

Exercise 4

1. Do the following :-

    a $\frac{2}{5}$ of 30 = (30 ÷ 5) x 2 = 6 x 2 = ...

    b $\frac{3}{4}$ of 24 = (24 ÷ ...) x 3 = ... x 3 = ...

    c $\frac{2}{3}$ of 18   d $\frac{4}{5}$ of 20   e $\frac{3}{8}$ of 40

    f $\frac{7}{10}$ of 100   g $\frac{2}{3}$ of 66   h $\frac{2}{9}$ of 27

    i $\frac{4}{9}$ of 63   j $\frac{3}{11}$ of 44   k $\frac{9}{10}$ of 80

    l $\frac{2}{5}$ of 35   m $\frac{2}{7}$ of 21   n $\frac{7}{8}$ of 56

    o $\frac{3}{4}$ of 400   p $\frac{3}{10}$ of 1000   q $\frac{4}{5}$ of 30

    r $\frac{4}{7}$ of 35   s $\frac{7}{10}$ of 60   t $\frac{5}{9}$ of 63

    u $\frac{5}{8}$ of 32   v $\frac{3}{5}$ of 35   w $\frac{9}{10}$ of 200.

2. a The ticket inspector on a train counted 36 passengers.

$\frac{3}{4}$ of the passengers were adults.

How many adults were on the train ?

b  A gardener has 30 rose bushes in his garden.

$\frac{2}{5}$ of them are red, $\frac{3}{10}$ are yellow and the rest are white.

(i) How many of the bushes are red ?

(ii) How many are white ?

3. a Which would you prefer to have :-

- a $\frac{4}{5}$ share in prize money winnings of £5500 or

- a $\frac{5}{7}$ share in a lottery win of £6300 ?

b  There are 365 days in a year. It rained on $\frac{3}{5}$ of them.

(i) On how many days did it rain ?

(ii) How many dry days were there ?

c A group of bird watchers spent a weekend on an island.

They counted 1800 birds, of which $\frac{1}{6}$ were from Europe,

$\frac{2}{9}$ were from South Africa, $\frac{5}{12}$ were from South America and the rest were local British birds.

List how many of the 1800 birds came from each area.

d  Mandy started the day with £200.

She spent $\frac{1}{4}$ of her money on the rail fare to London.

She spent $\frac{1}{5}$ of **what she had left** on her lunch.

She then spent $\frac{3}{8}$ of **what was remaining** on a new pair of shoes.

How much did Mandy then have left ?

Be able to add or subtract basic fractions.

If you had **one fifth** piece of pizza and someone gave you another **two fifths** of pizza you would have **three fifth** of the pizza.

This sum can be written as $\dfrac{1}{5} + \dfrac{2}{5} = \dfrac{3}{5}$.

Examples :-

$$\dfrac{1}{4} + \dfrac{2}{4} = \dfrac{3}{4}$$

$$\dfrac{4}{5} - \dfrac{1}{5} = \dfrac{3}{5}$$

$$\dfrac{9}{10} - \dfrac{6}{10} = \dfrac{3}{10}$$

Exercise 5

1. Find :-

 a $\dfrac{1}{3} + \dfrac{1}{3}$

 b $\dfrac{2}{5} + \dfrac{2}{5}$

 c $\dfrac{3}{10} + \dfrac{1}{10}$

 d $\dfrac{4}{7} + \dfrac{2}{7}$

 e $\dfrac{4}{5} - \dfrac{1}{5}$

 f $\dfrac{9}{10} - \dfrac{1}{10}$

 g $\dfrac{14}{15} - \dfrac{11}{15}$

 h $\dfrac{37}{100} - \dfrac{14}{100}$.

2. Find :-

 a $\dfrac{1}{2} + \dfrac{1}{2}$

 b $\dfrac{4}{5} + \dfrac{1}{5}$

 c $\dfrac{42}{100} + \dfrac{58}{100}$.

 Can you see that the answers to a, b and c are **one (1)** ?

3. I have 4 whole pizzas and a third of a pizza.

 Fern gave me another third of a pizza.

 How many pizzas do I have now ?

 $$4\dfrac{1}{3} + \dfrac{1}{3} = 4\dfrac{\cdots}{3}$$

     +

4. Find :- a $7\dfrac{1}{3} + \dfrac{1}{3}$

 b $9\dfrac{1}{4} + \dfrac{1}{4}$

 c $1\dfrac{3}{5} - \dfrac{1}{5}$

 d $3\dfrac{1}{2} + 2\dfrac{1}{2}$

 e $6\dfrac{3}{7} - 4\dfrac{2}{7}$

 f $7\dfrac{3}{4} - 5\dfrac{1}{4}$.

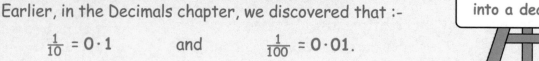

Changing Simple Fractions into Decimals

> Be able to change a basic fraction into a decimal.

Earlier, in the Decimals chapter, we discovered that :-

$\frac{1}{10} = 0\cdot1$ and $\frac{1}{100} = 0\cdot01$.

Notice from each of the diagrams that :-

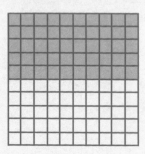 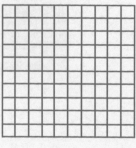 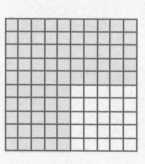

$\frac{1}{2} = \frac{50}{100} = 0\cdot50$, (or 0·5) $\frac{1}{4} = \frac{25}{100} = 0\cdot25$, $\frac{3}{4} = \frac{75}{100} = 0\cdot75$.

Exercise 6

1. For each diagram,

   (i) write each fraction (*out of 100*) and   (ii) the decimal it represents :-

a 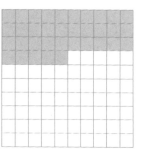   b 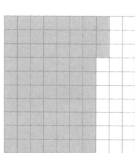   c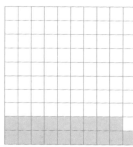

d 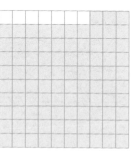   e 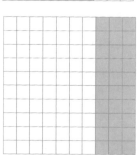   f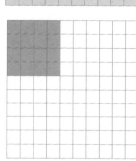

g 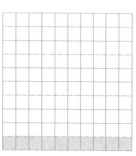   h 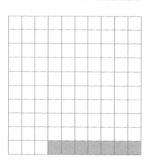   i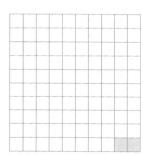

2. Write down what decimal fractions these represent, then list them in order with the **largest** decimal first :-

a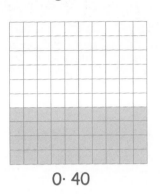

0· 40

b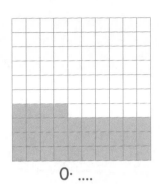

0· ....

c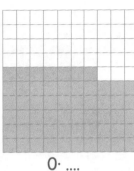

0· ....

d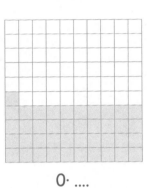

0· ....

e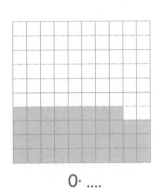

0· ....

f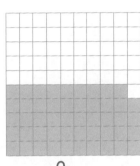

0· ....

3. Write these in order, **smallest** first :-

a   0· 70,   0·40,   0·35,   0·06,   0·91,   0·50

b   0·4,   0·74,   0·19,   0·2,   0·5,   0·6,   1·0

c   0·62, $\frac{1}{100}$,   0·34, $\frac{57}{100}$,   0·80, $\frac{76}{100}$

d   0·3, $\frac{1}{4}$,   0·74, $\frac{3}{4}$,   0·51, $\frac{1}{2}$,   0·07.

Fractions
Yipppeeeeeeee !

TeeJay Rules ok !

4. Write each of the following fractions as a decimal :-

a $\frac{63}{100}$ b $\frac{99}{100}$ c $\frac{8}{100}$ d $\frac{1}{10}$

e $\frac{1}{2}$ f $\frac{1}{4}$ g $\frac{3}{4}$ h $\frac{20}{50}$.

5. Write each of these decimals as a fraction :-

a   0·43   b   0·57   c   0·03   d   0·8.

1. a   What fraction of this shape is coloured red ?

    b   What fraction is **not** coloured red ?

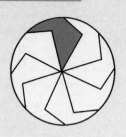

2. Write down any **three** fractions **equivalent** to $\frac{2}{5}$.

3. **Simplify** each of these fractions **as far as possible** :-

    a $\frac{6}{8}$ b $\frac{10}{12}$ c $\frac{15}{25}$ d $\frac{20}{24}$ e $\frac{36}{48}$ f $\frac{17}{51}$.

4. Find :-

    a $\frac{1}{3}$ of 18   b $\frac{1}{4}$ of 32   c $\frac{1}{8}$ of 160.

5. Find :-

    a $\frac{2}{3}$ of 24   b $\frac{3}{5}$ of 100   c $\frac{2}{7}$ of 77.

6. a   A grocer looked at the 60 apples in his barrel.

    $\frac{2}{5}$ of them had turned bad.

    How many apples was this ?

    b    At a wedding, there were 45 guests .

    $\frac{1}{3}$ of them were men and $\frac{3}{5}$ were women.

    The rest were children.

    (i)   How many women were at the wedding ?

    (ii) How many children were there ?

7. Find :-

    a $\frac{1}{4} + \frac{1}{4}$ b $\frac{1}{5} + \frac{3}{5}$ c $\frac{3}{7} + \frac{2}{7}$ d $\frac{5}{6} - \frac{1}{6}$

    e $\frac{7}{8} - \frac{3}{8}$ f $6\frac{3}{10} + \frac{3}{10}$ g $2\frac{2}{5} + 1\frac{1}{5}$ h $5\frac{7}{9} - 1\frac{2}{9}$.

8. Write as a decimal   a $\frac{1}{4}$ b $\frac{37}{100}$ c $\frac{9}{10}$.

Chapter 21

Statistics   Revision

Exercise 1

1. This pictograph shows the number of people waiting at a railway station one morning.

   a   How many people were at the station at :-

   (i)   7 am   (ii)   7.30 am

   (iii) 8.30 am   (iv)   9 am ?

   b   How many **more** people were there at 8 am than 7 am ?

   c   Suggest a reason why 8 am was the busiest time at the station.

   d   Give a reason why 7 am was not so busy .

   e   Why do you think the station was quieter at 9 am ?

Key:  stands for 5 people.

7 am	
7.30 am	
8 am	
8.30 am	
9 am	

2. An Indian Restaurant carried out a survey into which types of chicken dishes diners preferred.

   The results are shown in the **bar graph**.

   a   How many diners chose :-

   (i)   salsa   (ii)   tikka

   (iii) jalfrezi   (iv)   jaipuri ?

   b   What dish was liked by the fewest and how many chose it ?

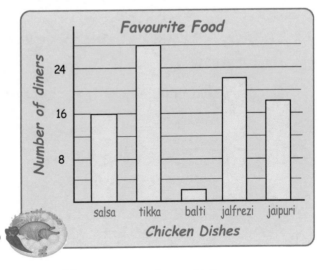

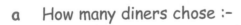

2. c   65 diners chose the all time favourite dish, chicken curry.
        It is not shown in the graph.

        Why would it be difficult to show this statistic ? Explain !

3. A survey was carried out at Blairdowdrie Nursery School
    as to which cartoons the children enjoy most.

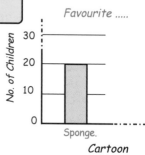

    The results are shown below.

SpongeBob	Tom & Jerry	Bugs Bunny	Scooby Doo	Mickey Mouse	Yogi Bear
60	70	75	90	10	15

    Use the given scale to draw a **bar chart** illustrating
    this information from the children.

Favourite .....

4. In a survey carried out outside Gordon's the Bakers last Saturday,
    people were asked to name their favourite pastry.

donuts	buns	eclairs	apple pie	muffins
buns	eclairs	muffins	donuts	donuts
donuts	buns	buns	buns	donuts
buns	muffins	donuts	buns	apple pie
buns	donuts	buns	muffins	eclairs
donuts	buns	apple pie	buns	muffins

    a   Draw a **frequency table** to show this information with the use of
        tally marks.

    b   Draw and label a neat **bar chart** to represent this information.

5. The information below shows the number of birthday cakes
    sold in Gordon's the Bakers the following week.

    | Mon - 36   Tue - 48   Wed - 24   Thu - 30   Fri - 36   Sat - 12. |

    Draw a **block graph** to show this information. (*Use each block as 6 cakes*).

Time Graphs

Be able to interpret a time (line) graph.

Time graphs can be used to compare values which change as time changes, (*seconds, minutes, hours, days, months, ...*).

Example :-

This time graph shows Jane's height from the age of 6 up to 16.

The yellow shaded line shows that when :-

• Jane was **10 years old**,

• she was **130 cm tall**.

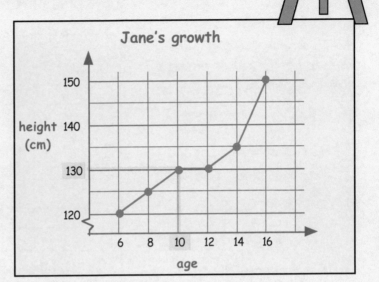

Exercise 2

1. Use the **time graph** above to answer the following :-

   a How tall was Jane at the age of :-   (i) 6   (ii) 12   (iii) 14 ?

   b How old was Jane when she was 150 cm tall ?

   c How old was Jane when she was 125 cm tall ?

   d Estimate the height of Jane at 15 years of age.

2. This time graph shows the number of pay per view films bought from a TV company during one week.

   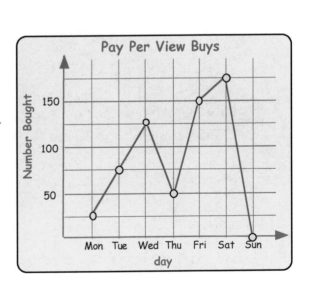

   a How many films were bought on :-

      (i) Wednesday   (ii) Friday ?

   b How many more films were bought on Friday than on Tuesday ?

   c Between which 2 days was there the largest rise in film sales ?

2. d Which is the most popular day to buy films ?

   e Why do you think this day was the most popular ?

   f Give a possible reason for the Sunday figure that week.

3. The time graph shows the
   number of cars that passed
   over the Golden Gate Bridge
   on Friday.

   a How many cars passed
      over the bridge between :–

      (i)   5 am and 6 am

      (ii) 7 am and 8 am

      (iii) 9 am and 10 am

      (iv) 11 am and noon

      (v)   noon and 1 pm ?

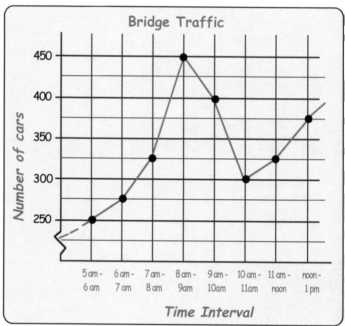

   b During what time interval did 450 cars
      pass over the bridge ?

   c During what time interval did 300 cars
      pass over the bridge ?

   d Between what two time intervals was
      there the biggest **increase** in traffic ?

   e Why do you think the traffic was busiest between 8 am and 9 am ?

   f How many more cars crossed the bridge between
      8 am and 9 am than 10 am to 11 am ?

   g How many cars in total crossed the bridge between 6 am and noon ?

   h *Optional group exercise.*

      Investigate how many cars pass your school gate during a particular
      one hour spell. (The teacher will choose an appropriate time).

4. The time graph shows the ice cream sales (in 100's) from *Tony's Van* from Feb to Nov 2014.

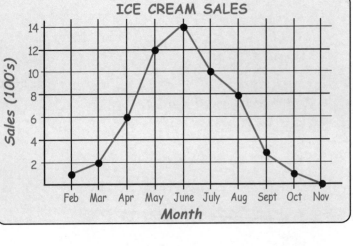

ICE CREAM SALES

a How many ice creams did Tony sell in April? (in 100's)

b How many ice creams did Tony sell in :-

   (i) March   (ii) June   (iii) September?

c By how much did the sales **increase** between May and June?

d Between which two **consecutive** months did sales :-

   (i) rise the most?   (ii) fall the most?

e How many ice creams did Tony sell altogether from April to August?

f Why do you think the sales go up and down in this way?

5. The **comparative** time graph shows the sales from two different car showrooms, Alfie Clarke and **Reg Hardy**.

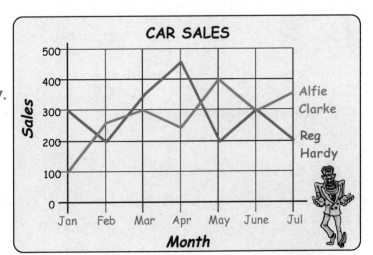

CAR SALES

a Which company had the better sales in :-

   (i) February

   (ii) April

   (iii) May

   (iv) June?

b How many cars were sold by each company in :-

   (i) May   (ii) March   (iii) April?

c Over the months shown, which company had the better (**total**) sales?

1. Teachers were asked to name their favourite city.

    The results are shown in the bar chart.

    a   How many teachers voted :-

        (i)   London   (ii) Delhi

        (iii) Rome   (iv) in total ?

    b   How many more teachers preferred Rome to Madrid ?

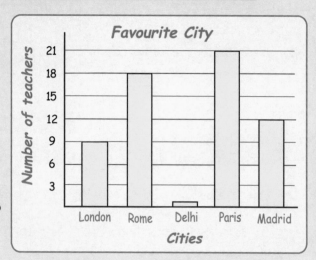

2. Children were asked which day they preferred to have a school meal.

    The results, showing which days, are as shown :-

    | Mon - 12 | Tue - 10 | Wed - 26 | Thu - 18 | Fri - 16. |

    Draw a bar chart to show this information.

3. A store recorded the number of laptops sales using the time graph shown.

    a   How many were sold in :-

        (i)   Sept   (ii) Dec

        (iii) Feb   (iv) altogether ?

    b   How many more laptops were sold in December rather than in October ?

    c   Why do you think sales were so high in November and December ?

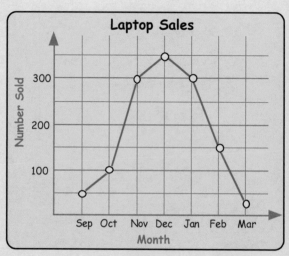

1. Write out the number 9204 fully **in words**.

2. Write the number five thousand six hundred and ninety **using digits**.

3. Rearrange the numbers given below in order, starting with the **smallest**.

    7081   8070   8002   7718   8018   8081.

4. What numbers are represented by **A, B, C** and **D** on the given scales ?

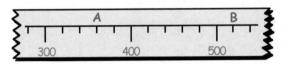 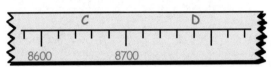

5. What number lies **halfway** between 2500 and 6500 ?

6. Write down the number that is 2000 **less than** 7300.

7. Write down the next two numbers each time :-

    a   685,   690,   695,   ..., ...   b   320,   310,   300,   ..., ...

    c   9600,   9400,   9200,   ..., ...   d   9000,   8500,   8000,   ..., ...

8. a   Change to number form :-   **(i)** XIV   **(ii)** LXXXV **(iii)** XLVII.

    b   Change to Roman numerals :-   **(i)** 18   **(ii)** 37   **(iii)** 84.

9. How many lines of symmetry do each of these shapes have ?

    a   b   c   d

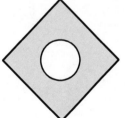 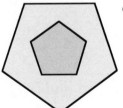  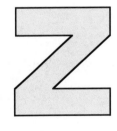

10. **Trace** or **copy** this shape and draw
    the other half so the red dotted line
    is a line of symmetry.

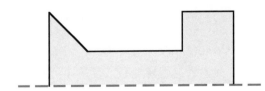

11. Set down and then work out :-

a   5375
    + 3938

b   7438 – 2962

c   6785
    + 888

d   10 000
    – 1836

12. There were 3871 Liverton supporters and 1965 Everpool supporters at a local football derby.

a   How many were there **altogether** at the match ?

b   How many **more** Liverton than Everpool supporters were at the match ?

13. Do the following **mentally** (*no working should be seen*) :-

a   39 + 55

b   249 + 49

c   5200 + 2600

d   91 – 19

e   2600 – 550

f   10 000 – 3800

g   2035 + 1999

h   3000 – 29.

14. Round to the :-

a   nearest **10** :-   (i)   94   (ii)   377   (iii)   805.

b   nearest **100** :- (i)   439   (ii)   3816   (iii)   9268.

c   nearest **1000** :- (i)   2736   (ii)   6085   (iii)   9 500.

15. Change these times to **24 hour** format :-

a   4.55 am   b   3.10 in the afternoon   c   25 to 11 at night.

16. Write the following in **12 hour** format :-   (*remember to use **am** or **pm***)

a   0935   b   1420   c   1045   d   2050.

17. How many **minutes** are between :-

a   5.30 pm and 7 pm   b   midnight and 0120   c   1240 and 1335 ?

18. a   How many days are there in :- (i)   August   (ii)   November ?

b   How many months are there in 3 years ?

c   How many days are there from the 26th of March to the 5th of April, including both dates ?

19. **Copy** and **complete** :-

    a   8 x 7 = ...   **b**   5 x 10 = ...   **c**   9 x 9 = ...

    d   7 x 6 = ...   **e**   11 x 1 = ...   **f**   3 x 5 x 6 = ...

20. What numbers are missing ?

    a   6 x .... = 42   **b**   .... x 8 = 400   **c**   .... x 9 = 63

    d   .... x 10 = 110   **e**   7 x .... = 4900   **f**   .... x 5 = 0.

21. **Copy** and **complete** these multiplications :-

    a   76   **b**   308   **c**   276
        x 8   x 9   x 6

    d   357   **e**   829   **f**   234
       x 5   x 10   x 7

22. A container holds a **gross (144)** of Nesbury's small Easter egg.

    Tadsco buys in **8 gross** of eggs.

    How many eggs is this ?

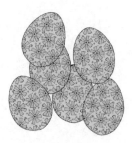

23. State what temperatures are represented on these thermometers :-

    a

-10°C   -5°C   0°C   5°C   10°C

    b

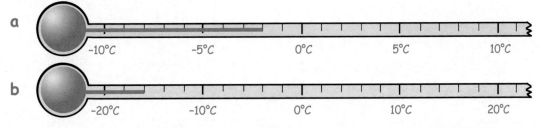

-20°C   -10°C   0°C   10°C   20°C

24. What is the temperature :-

    a   3°C up from 15°C   **b**   6°C down from 6°C

    c   5°C up from -8°C   **d**   10°C down from 7°C ?

25. Which integer is **halfway** between :-

    a   10 and 16   **b**   -8 and 8   **c**   -2 and -12 ?

26. **Copy** and **complete** :-

   a   9)45   b   8)64   c   9)117   d   7)126

   e   5)345   f   10)670   g   4)256   h   9)306.

27. Write in the form 8)96   and work out the answer :-

   a   96 ÷ 8   b   9 into 63   c   112 divided by 7

   d $\dfrac{384}{6}$ e   395 ÷ 5   f   10 into 7200.

28. Nine biscuits weigh 558 grams. What is the weight of 1 biscuit ?

29. George and his 7 workmates share a lottery prize of £576.

   How much money will each receive ?

30. **Copy** the coordinate grid shown opposite.

   a   Write down the coordinates of point P.

   b   Plot the 3 points **A**(0, 6), **B**(2, 8) and **C**(7, 3).

   D is a point to be put on the grid so that figure **ABCD** is a **rectangle**.

   c   On your diagram plot the point **D** and write down its coordinates.

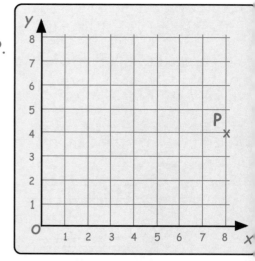

31. What decimal number is represented by this diagram ?

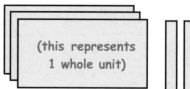

(this represents 1 whole unit)

32. Draw diagrams (similar to Question 31) to represent :-   a   2·5   b   1·74.

33. In the decimal number 63·85, what does the :-

   a   6 represent   b   5 represent   c   8 represent ?

34. Write down the number that is :-

   a   0·3 up from 6·8   **b**   0·05 down from 4·87   **c** $\frac{3}{10}$ down from 8·3.

35. What number is **halfway** between :-

   a   0·3 and 0·7   **b**   4·4 and 5·0   **c**   0·52 and 0·58 ?

36. **a**   Arrange in order, **smallest** first :-   2·8,   2·19,   2·58,   3,   2·29,   2·12.

     b   Arrange in order, **largest** first :-   3·64,   3·7,   4·51,   4·07,   5·8,   4·02.

37. To what decimal numbers are the arrows pointing ?

  a

  b
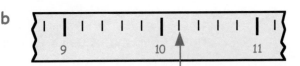

38. This triangle can be described as follows :-

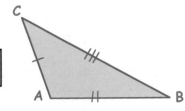

> Triangle **ABC** is an **obtuse angled scalene** triangle.

Name and describe both of these triangles **fully** :-

  a
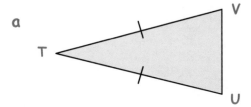
  b
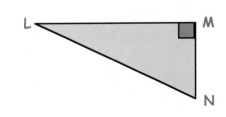

39. Round the following to **the nearest whole number** :-

   a   5·4   **b**   8·9   **c**   63·48   **d**   67·73.

40. Do the following **mentally** (*no working*) :-

   a   2·7 + 7·1   **b**   9·2 + 5·68   **c**   8·7 – 2·5   **d**   0·64 – 0·58.

41. Copy the following and find :-

a	**b**	**c**	**d**
3·82	35·54	10·8	15·65
+ 2·49	+ 6·72	– 6·3	– 9·87

41. e   £3·87 + £4·95   f   £24·48 + £5·32   g   £5·63 – £2·87

    h   45·42 – 9·73   i   30 – 2·45   j   85·7 – 38·49.

42. Harry buys a pair of trousers for £24·99
    and a belt for £12·49.

    How much change should he receive from £40 ?

43. a   Write down the meaning of the word **quadrilateral**.

    b   Name 6 different types of quadrilaterals.

44. True (T) or False (F) ?

    a   A rhombus is made up of 2 identical isosceles triangles.

    b   The opposite sides of a parallelogram are equal in length.

    c   A kite has only 1 line of symmetry.

    d   A rectangle fits into its outline 4 ways if you can turn it and rotate it.

    e   A square has exactly 8 lines of symmetry.

45. Write down 2 ways in which a **parallelogram** is different from a **rhombus**.

46. Name the polygon which has 5 sides.

47. What is a **regular** polygon ?

48. Write each of these amounts using a decimal point :-

    a    b    c

49. Find:-

    a   £28·45   b   £207·86   c   £26·32 – £19·59   d   £111·21 + £19·89
        + £ 14·37   – £92·58

50. a   Eric spent £13·49 and gave a £20 note. How much change did he get ?

    b   Alice got £11·85 change from two £20 notes. How much had she spent ?

51. How many :-

    a   minutes in 4 hours   b   seconds in five mins. c   weeks in a year ?

52. How many days are there in :-

    a   January   b   June   c   February 2020 ?

53. Change each of these to **minutes** and **seconds** :-

    a   80 secs   b   210 secs   c   1201 secs.

54. Change each of these to **hours** and **minutes** :-

    a   100 mins   b   250 mins   c   500 mins.

55. Change each of these from **minutes** and **seconds** to **seconds** :-

    a   1 mins 55 secs   b   4 mins 20 secs   c   10 mins 10 secs.

56. Change each of these from **hours** and **minutes** to **minutes** :-

    a   1 hr 25 mins   b   3 hrs 20 mins   c   5 hrs 55 mins.

57. Copy and complete :-

    a   2 mins 15 secs   b   8 mins 50 secs   c   3 hrs 20 mins
        + 5 mins 40 secs   – 3 mins 35 secs   – 1 hr   30 mins

58. Write down the answer to each of these :-

    a   240 x 10   b   35 x 100   c   9 x 1000   d   910 ÷ 10

    e   5000 ÷ 100   f   8000 ÷ 1000 g   7 x 11   h   12 x 10

    i   99 ÷ 11   j   132 ÷ 12   k   156 ÷ 12   l   231 ÷ 11.

59. Paperclips come in boxes of 100.

    A school bought in 15 boxes.

    How many paperclips was that ?

60. Eggs are sometimes packed in boxes of a **dozen** (12).

In a supermarket, there are 5 rows with four boxes of eggs in each row.

How many eggs is that altogether ?

61. 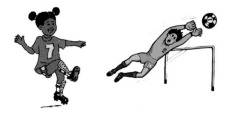 In a school football tournament, there are 132 players formed into teams of 11 each.

How many teams is that ?

62. Change :-

    a   3 cm 8 mm to mm   **b**   1800 mm to cm   **c**   76 mm to cm & mm

    d   7 m 25 cm to cm   **e**   470 cm to m & cm   **f**   4 km 600 m to m

    g   6750 m to km & m   **h**   5 m to mm   **i** $1\frac{1}{2}$ km to m.

63. Change :-

    a   4 litres 200 ml to ml   **b**   3600 ml to L & ml   **c** $5\frac{1}{4}$ litres to ml.

64. Change :-

    a   8 kg 350 g to g   **b**   7200 g to kg & g   **c** $6\frac{3}{4}$ kg to g.

65. Find the perimeter of the rectangle and the square.

    a  7 cm   **b** 13·5 cm

    18 cm

66. Write down the area of this shape in **cm²** .

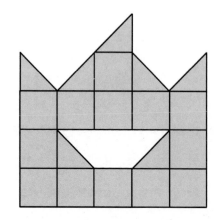